Strength Training for Fencers

by Harry James

SKA SwordPlay Books

SwordPlay Books

www.swordplaybooks.com
Publishers of

Zbigniew Czajkowski
Understanding Fencing

Sergei Golubitsky
Fencing Is My Life

Aladar Kogler, Ph.D.
One Touch at a Time: Psychological Processes in Fencing
2nd Edition, Revised and Enlarged

Istvan Lukovich
Fencing: The Modern International Style
and
Electric Foil Fencing

Laszlo Szabo
Fencing and the Master

Imre Vass
Epee Fencing: A Complete System

Distributors of
Jean-Jacques Gillet
Foil Technique and Terminology

Published by
SKA SwordPlay Books
3939 Victory Boulevard
Staten Island, NY 10314
Phone: 1.718.761.3305
Fax: 1.800.361.1379
E-mail: skhinoy@si.rr.com
www.swordplaybooks.com

Contents

Contents

Index of Illustrations

Index of Illustrations

List of Tables

Dedication

This book is dedicated to Arthur Blumert. In 1963 he convinced the Somerville High School Athletic Director to allow him to start a fencing team by promising never to take a salary for coaching. Years later, when later athletic directors begged him to take one, he refused. In 1975, I joined the team and started a long and happy fencing career. Later Mr. Blumert retired after leading Somerville fencing for 27 years. Years later he was inducted into the Somerville High Athletic Hall of Fame. During his acceptance speech he said, "I've always said, if you live long enough, someone will give you an award." He went to God in the summer of 2004.

Thanks

Thanks to Rosemary, Harry and Molly for a lifetime of love and help. Thanks to God and the Saints for sustaining me inwardly. Thanks to Ralph Bellantoni for being a fencing pal. Thanks to my biology teachers, particularly Len Martin of Somerville High School and Lee Pollack of Drew University, for helping me perfect my scientific reasoning. Thanks to my fencing coaches, Art Blumert of Somerville High and Paul Primamore of Drew University, for teaching me this great sport. Thanks to Dave Cowell, a political science professor at Drew, for telling me I could be a writer. Thanks to Somerville High for supporting the sport of fencing for over 40 years. Thanks to Dr. Dave Lisneski for answers to functional anatomy questions. Thanks to all the great coaches who have helped me along the way, Al Peters, Mark Holbrow, Michel Sebastiani, and Alex Beguinet. Thanks to my colleagues in New Jersey High School Fencing for their help and friendship. Thanks to the fencers I have coached for sharing the sport I love. Thanks to SwordPlay Books editor Steve Khinoy for helping me get this book straightened out and published.

Special thanks to Art Blumert's kids for digging up pictures of Art running a fencing program for the "Forgotten Bastards of Iceland" during his service in World War 2. I wish God's blessing for you and yours.

Credits

Photography: Harry James
Fitness Models: Molly James, Ralph Bellantoni, Harry James.
Cover Photo: Birgit Roy
Back Cover Photo of Harry James: Molly James
Cover Design: Harry James

How to Use This Book

This book lays out exercises for fencers at each stage of their physical development. In addition, it lays out the rationale for weight training, the rationale for each exercise, the theory of progression from one exercise to another, and illustrated instructions for each exercise. The first half of the book explains how the body develops physically during the course of an exercise program. The second half of the book explains how to develop the body in the best possible way by exposing it to a good exercise program. Finally, the book explains how to use a strength training program during the fencing season.

For General Fitness Readers

First, I want to heartily welcome the general fitness reader who has come upon this book. The values of fitness for the sport of fencing are very similar to the values of the general fitness reader. You want to be strong, quick and agile, and so does the competitive fencer. You should first look at the outline of the theory of progression found at the beginning of Section 2. Then look through the exercises explained and illustrated in the next three chapters. These three chapters show you the wide variety of exercises that will help you maintain your interest in working out. You are in it for the long run, and these exercises will help you stay the course. Then go back and read the safety and theory in Chapters 1 – 3 so you know why you do what you do. Then start with Phase1 and work your way up, filling in any deficits as you go.

For Coaches

If you are a coach, you should ground yourself in the theory of weight training and physical development. For example, when you understand the parameters of exercise found in Chapter 3. you will understand why a fencer is being stressed during any physical activity. In addition, you should ground yourself in the theory of progression outlined at the beginning of Section 2 and elucidated throughout Section 2. You can then identify the level of progression of each of your fencers, spot their physical liabilities, and set them on a path to physical improvement. A knowledge of theory will also help you select from the array of exercises in Section 2 the ones you would like to put in your program and then study each exercise so as to be able to instruct your athletes. The chapter on safety is also critical so you can do your best to keep your program running injury-free. Finally, you can make use of the sections in Chapter 7 on how to organize a training year.

First, ground yourself in safety principles. Then learn the theory behind weight training.

For Beginners in Strength Training

If you are a beginner who has no experience with weight training, you *must* read the chapter on safety. You should also read Chapter 3 because it tells you important things like how to figure out how much weight to lift and how many times to lift it. To start out, you should first concentrate on Phase 1 and become really good at the exercises in that phase. You should consider getting personal instruction in the basic lifts and lifting techniques. Then follow the phases on up.

Read the chapter on safety.

For Experienced Athletes

If you are an athlete who has already done some weightlifting, *review the safety chapter* even though you think you know the principles it covers. You should also become familiar with the theory of progression of exercises outlined at the beginning of Section 2 and elucidated throughout Section 2. Finally, learn how to organize your training year as explained in Section 2, Phase 4, the chapter on the "Incorporate" phase.

For Older Fencers

You may have to become a beginner again.

If you are an older fencer trying to continue with your sport in the midst of family and job responsibilities, this book can help you. You may have unknowingly lost some of the physical attributes you gained, perhaps without too much thought, when you were younger. *Review the chapter on safety* so you can avoid common mishaps. Read Section 1, Chapters 2 and 3 about the way the body builds itself up for sport. Then read the outline of the theory of progression at the beginning of Section 2. After this, you may need to admit that through lack of physical training you have become a beginner again in some of your physical abilities. In that case, start at Phase 1 and work to fill in your deficits as you progress through the exercises and the phases.

Remember, your body doesn't improve as quickly as it did when you were younger. Be patient and don't rush things.

Introduction

Many of us remember the training regimens that we learned 25 years ago from gym teachers, drill sergeants, or weightlifting heroes like Arnold Schwarzenegger and Franco Columbu. But these are no longer sufficient for most athletes. We live in a new world of athletic possibilities—possibilities of strength and speed that are fashioned to meet the unique needs of our sport.

Bodybuilders inspired many people to take up weight training. When I was a kid, my friends and I all wanted to get strong. So we put together our weight benches and our barbells and lifted weights according to the prescriptions in books like Arnold's *The Encyclopedia of Modern Bodybuilding* and Franco's *Weight Training and Bodybuilding.*

We pumped a lot of iron—or cement, if we were using those cement-filled plastic weights. We had a lot of fun. The camaraderie and physical exhilaration of weightlifting improved our young lives. My fencing buddies and I also hoped it would help our fencing. I'm sure it helped a bit. But I wish I knew then what I know now about physical training!

In my experience, fencers have historically avoided the weight room. My first coach told me weightlifting would make me stiff and slow. If it did, that was only because my training techniques were poor. If you practice *modern* strength-training techniques, you will be faster, not slower.

Fencers are not bodybuilders! They need a workout program that *begins* with basic weight-lifting techniques, then veers away from basic strength exercises into modern, *sports*-oriented exercise. The most complicated function that a bodybuilder must perform is to stand on a stage and selectively tense a muscle. Fencers need a program that prepares them to perform complex functions on a constantly changing stage.

Fencers are not bodybuilders.

I can not guarantee that strength training will make you fence better. I promise that, if you are healthy, it will make your biomechanical machine function at a higher level. You will feel fitter and stronger. Modern fencing is extremely athletic. You are unlikely to succeed without finely honed physical fitness.

This book explains the science behind the strategy for developing a strong body fit for fencing. It introduces you to the essential tools of modern strength training. And it shows you how to do a wide variety of modern strength training exercises.

Bodybuilding has *one long phase* with many variations. Modern *athletic* training has *four* major phases. These four phases provide the basic organizing principle of this book and the underlying pattern of a good strength training program. I call the four phases Separate! Integrate! Accelerate! and Incorporate!

The four phases of strength training.

- *Separate* the muscles and the motions and work them to rehabilitate the weak ones and add drive and energy to all.
- *Integrate* the individual muscles and motions into chains of force that begin to approximate certain aspects of sports movements.
- *Accelerate* the joints and limbs to produce speed and power in the chains of force.
- *Incorporate* the strength and power gained in strength training sessions into the skills necessary for success in athletic competition.

Separate!

Bodybuilding begins and ends in the *Separate!* phase. Bodybuilders isolate a muscle, then work it so that it is stimulated to grow. Bodybuilders have no need of getting one of their muscles to work with any others, except that they must stand on a stage and selectively tense their muscles. Getting the muscles to work with each other comes in the second phase: *Integrate!* Bodybuilders have no need to *Accelerate* their limbs quickly and move them at high speeds. And they have no need to *Incorporate!* the movement and strength they've learned in strength training into a complex discipline like striking a moving ball—or defeating a wily opponent who is moving at high speed. I don't mean to insult bodybuilders here. Natural bodybuilding takes tremendous discipline and dedication and is deserving of respect in my opinion. But most athletes must go beyond the *Separate!* phase outlined in most traditional strength training books and begin to use a four phase program. This book will tell you the reasoning behind the four phases and show you how to implement them.

Integrate!
Accelerate!
Incorporate!

This book doesn't cover cardio fitness— but cardio fitness is essential for fencers.

A note of caution here: There are some important topics that this book doesn't cover. Cardiovascular fitness is one of them. It's obviously important to fencing. It doesn't matter how strong you are if you're sucking wind after the first two minutes of a three-minute bout. But cardiovascular fitness would require a whole separate book. Other important topics that I won't discuss in any detail are diet, rest and recovery, kinesiology, and psychological preparation. This book focuses on strength training.

We had a lot of fun with the old training methods we used when we were kids. I still think kindly of Arnold and Franco and their training books. *But modern training is even more fun!* There are more things to do in the training room these days besides hoisting iron: more challenges, more skills, more laughs and friendship as you struggle to get the exercises right and get a peak performance from your body. The road to sports success is more fun than it has ever been. I wish you a lot of enjoyment in the journey and some satisfying sports successes along the way.

Section 1:   The Principles

1. Training Safely

> *Before you do anything that is mentioned in this book, get advice and approval from a licensed medical professional. The exercises discussed in these pages may be too strenuous for you. You may have a hidden medical condition that would make these exercises inappropriate for you at this time. Don't assume you know what is going on with your body. Get professional medical advice before beginning any exercise program.*

You can't rush Mother Nature

Consider all the things that are growing in your body as a result of your exercise program: blood vessels, nerves, connective tissue, muscle tissue, bones. It only takes a brief moment of calculation to realize that, like Rome, your new body will not be built in a day. You must work through all the steps of the program and you must not rush any of the steps.

If you try to rush the process, you risk injury, both in the gym and in sports competition. Your connective tissue and your bones develop much, much more slowly than nerve pathways and muscles (connective tissue takes 5 – 7 times longer to develop than muscle tissue). Therefore, developing your muscles too fast risks injury to bone and connective tissue.

A rushed lifting program can cause injury instead of preventing it. You can produce muscles that are wired up for big bursts of effort before your connective tissue is strong enough to hold your parts together. If in this situation you get a rush of adrenaline and try to yank a big weight or fire off some outrageous move on the fencing strip, you can "pop a gasket" that will sit you down for weeks or months.

Let me tell you the story of a friend of mine. He was a strong and energetic man, but he had never participated in sports or lifted weights. He was a doctor during the week and liked to do carpentry on the weekends. He was proud of the fact that he looked good even though he didn't work out. God gave him the genes for nice muscles. At age 50, he decided to try working out. He hired a personal trainer. He liked the burst of energy he got from lifting. He became an avid lifter.

Danger! Don't rush your training.

But just two months into his program, he used poor form on a lat pulldown (behind his neck rather than in front of his chest), pulled too great a weight and ruptured a disk in his neck. He needed vertebral fusion and is now permanently weak in one arm.

I have no idea what his trainer had told him. Perhaps she just gave him tragically bad advice. Or perhaps he thought he knew better than the trainer he'd hired. But if *you* are responsible for someone's training program, you have to instruct your students to go slowly. If they refuse to listen to you, you should refuse to train them. For people who really get into it, lifting can be like a drug. It can draw an athlete to take on more and heavier loads for the fun of it, for the exhilaration of it. If you're the one in training, you must use your head. Stick with the program rather than letting the "rush" convince you to do dangerous things.

Consider the athletes who call themselves power lifters. They mature and reach their competitive peak in their 30's. Other athletes are put out to pasture in their 30's, but power lifters need that many years to build their bodies to the point where they can do the incredible things they do.

Fred Hatfield, who co-founded ISSA (the certification program that got me started in physical training) trained for 30 years to get to his peak. He weighed 255 pounds at his competitive peak and broke the then world record by loading 1014 pounds on his back, bending his knees so his thighs were horizontal, then standing back up. He squatted more than half a ton! People like Dr. Hatfield prove the value of patient and faithful labor. You can make your body stronger and fitter for fencing if you patiently work the program. If you don't rush, you just might get somewhere.

The same goes for your training session: *don't rush into it!* Before training, be sure to warm up well with some light jogging or calisthenics. When you are done working, cool down with a little easy stretching.

Youth Training

"*Your life will be longer than you think. At your age, you tend to live like your life is almost over. And you feel like if you don't have something now you are in grave danger of never getting it. But this impression is false. You have a lot of time. Work hard. Have faith. Don't panic.*"

That's what I tell my teenage athletes. It's hard for them to listen.

First through sixth grades—take it easy.

We can think of first grade through sixth grade as the first of two major age groups for youth sports. When training children this young, coaches should not prescribe heavy lifting because it can damage children's joints. Similarly, we should avoid training in extremes of heat and humidity because children's thermoregulatory systems are not well developed: they sweat less, create more heat per body mass, and adapt to heat more slowly. We should also avoid training too hard or too long because the young athletes are still growing. It's all too easy for them to develop stress fractures, overuse and repetitive use injuries, and damage to developing joint surfaces. Children don't need a huge input of exercise to make their muscles grow. Extremes of exhaustion may change their growth pattern. Exercise strengthens them because of neuromuscular learning, not because their muscles get bigger.

Kids in this early age group need exercise so that they can experiment with and begin to develop a wide range of skills in a low-pressure environment. They need exercise to develop a good self-image. They need exercise to learn to enjoy their bodies, enjoy the process of skill development and the camaraderie of sport, and enjoy physical exertion itself. They need sport to learn the morals of fair play, sportsmanship and teamwork. Remember we are working with eternal souls, and young hearts, minds and bodies. These kids are not here to make our reputations. We are here to help them grow.

The second half of the youth scale runs from seventh through twelfth grade. This is the stage where kids are growing from childhood toward adulthood. At the beginning, all of the suggestions and precautions for first through sixth grades still apply to them. Then, as they grow, we advance them toward adult levels of training.

Transitional stage— strength training with light weights to learn the skills.

Here are some specifics for athletes in these in-between ages. If they are still growing, heavy lifting and the most demanding forms of plyometrics (for example, depth jumping) are not helpful. (For a fuller discussion of plyometrics, see p. 117 ff.) However, they should lift light weights to master the many diverse skills of strength training. *Lifting at the beginning of this age range is more for skill learning than muscle building.* The Committee on Sports Medicine and Fitness of the American Academy of Pediatrics recommends that resistance exercises should be practiced with *no load* until the exercise skill has been mastered. However, from my studies in the literature on motor learning, I have come to the conclusion that it is hard to learn a load-carrying skill without some load. So I suggest that young people learn the skills with a light load.

Even though these preteens and teens have thermoregulatory systems that are more advanced than those of very young children, it is still not good for them to be made to work in extreme heat. Extreme heat frequently encountered will shorten the athletic careers even of adults. Unfortunately, the attitude that "the show must go on" still prevails, and even young athletes are made to train and compete in truly harrowing climatic conditions. In the case of fencing, remember, too, that fencers wear a lot of extra clothing! Also avoid extremely high exercise intensity and duration. The best athletes are not necessarily those that survive the most brutal training regimens.

Don't train in extreme heat!

Throughout grades seven through twelve, psychological pressure on the young athlete increases. Care of the athletes' hearts and minds must continue in earnest. The coach must care for the person inside the competitor and mold people who value fair play, sportsmanship and teamwork. Your athletes will go beyond their athletic careers and become spouses and parents, workers and employers, politicians, ministers, doctors and the like. As coaches, we should hope they use the determination and work ethic that they learned in sports to raise healthy and loving families, bring about peace, save souls and discover cures for diseases. But there's much less chance of that if what they learned in their sports career was to cheat and disrespect their fellow human beings.

*Care for the **person** inside the **competitor.***

Training Women

Athletic women have more injuries than their male counterparts and women in general suffer more than men from painful conditions such as headaches. This pain and injury comes from two sources: joint instability and postural problems.

People who are very flexible have more problems with instability of joints and therefore more strains, sprains and all out tears of joints. Women are in general more flexible than men are, so they are more likely to be unstable. *The basic solution to this problem is strength training.* Women's passive stability systems (ligaments, tendons and so on) provide less stability, so their active stability systems (muscles and nerves) must be taught to provide more of their stability.

Instability in both Men and Women

In both men and women, instability in the body leads to postural problems stemming from the normal stresses and strains of life and athletics. The neck and shoulders are functionally one unit, but in our society, neck and shoulder posture —and low back posture as well—tend to be bad. Computers, cars and books on tables conspire to make us round our shoulders and lean our heads forward. And while we're trying to develop those six-pack abs, too many crunches round our shoulders and make our heads crane forward. It is said that for every inch your head leans forward, its effective weight on your neck muscles is doubled.

More flexibility = more instability.

And there's more. Sitting all day destabilizes the pelvis and makes the muscles connected to it (the front and rear leg muscles, gluteus muscles, hip adductor and abductor muscles and front, rear and side trunk muscles) unbalanced and uncoordinated. The pelvis is the foundation of the structure of the spine. If the foundation is tilted or unstable, the structure above it will experience many stresses and incur damage in the long run. And if the athlete puts weights on the top of a stressed structure with a poor foundation, imagine how much faster the damage will occur!

15

> **It is extremely rare that an athlete will have no postural deficits. Athletes must correct postural problems at the very beginning of their strength training program and keep track of posture as the program progresses.**

Strength Standards for Women

*Women: Try for the same strength standards as men when your body weight provides the resistance—**it's your body!***

It is not uncommon to hear someone suggest that women should be given a lower standard of strength (for instance, in lower abdominal exercises or push-ups), because of differences in physiology. I know of no good reason why women should accept lower basic standards than men, and one good reason why women should aspire to the same basic standard: *It is their body!* They must be able to handle their body safely and effectively in a sports combat situation.

This does not mean that women should try to keep up with men in the weight room. You may respond more slowly to training than men. You may be behind men of your own age and training maturity when you begin training. You may never attain the same peak strength as men. But for exercises in which your own body weight provides the resistance, there should be no difference. Your legs are *your* legs—no matter how light or heavy they are, you must learn to control them through the lower abdominal exercises. Your shoulders are *your* shoulders—you must make them strong enough to handle the power your body can put through them in a pushup from the toes.

In a nutshell, most women *need* strength training more than most men do. They need this whole program. And their coaches need to be doubly sure that the women they coach do not move past the basics without developing a firm foundation of good posture, good form, and good stability strength. All of their joints must track correctly on every repetition of the exercises. Their posture must be correct for every repetition of the exercises. (I am not suggesting for a moment that coaches can afford to be lax with the form of their male athletes. There is simply *more* reason to be a perfectionist with women, because experience shows women athletes to be more prone to injury and pain.)

Keeping Track of Over-training / Under-resting Syndrome

Everyone starts the season with high hopes, high enthusiasm, and high energy. As the season comes to a close and the last and sometimes biggest competitions loom, many on the team have a little less hop in their step, a little less hunger to practice and a little more doubt about their ability to win. And if there is no off-season, the foot-dragging, sour-faced approach to sport may become a year-round condition.

This is called over-training syndrome. I like to call it over-training/under-resting syndrome because, for most athletes, the problem is too little resting and nutrition, not too much training. Most young athletes I know are doing a good bit of so many things that it all adds up to doing too much. They must rest and eat well if they want to be healthy.

Walking the tightrope: balancing between too much and too little

But there is a problem with this necessary piece of advice: there is a high correlation between hours spent training and performance in competition. According to one study, athletes in the top 20 in their sport in the world spend on average over 1,000 hours per year in training (including both sport-specific training and physical conditioning). Athletes competing on the international level spend roughly 800 hours per year in training. Athletes competing on the national level spend roughly 600 hours per year in training. Athletes vying for a state championship spend roughly 400 hours per year in training.

During the competitive season, athletes on my high school team train 2 hours a day, 5 days a week for 12 weeks. This totals 120 hours of training. If, in the 40-week off-season, they devote about seven and a half hours a week to strength training and endurance straining, as well as fencing, they'll be up at that 400-hour state championship level—with two weeks off for recovery. And it doesn't seem unreasonable to put in that kind of time, especially when you're young.

The problem is that when you train, you need more rest and nutrition. And rest and nutrition take time. And the remainder of a young athlete's week may be crammed with work, school, clubs, recreation and social life. Many young athletes are tempted to skip rest, skip active recovery like massage, and skip meals—all too "save time." Sooner or later, this will surely result in over-training syndrome.

Don't skip meals or recovery periods.

Don't neglect nutrition.

What are the signs of over-training syndrome? Over-training is not simple fatigue. Fatigue happens after every workout, and a healthy athlete eats, sleeps, and feels better in a day or two. Over-training syndrome is the result of many bouts of fatigue followed by inadequate rest and recovery. When their bodies and minds experience this cumulative lack of recovery, people begin to come apart at the edges. In the psychological realm, they show increased excitability and reduced concentration, seem more irrational and sensitive to criticism, tend to isolate themselves, lack initiative, confidence, will power, and fighting power, fear competition, easily give up on tactical plans, and seem depressed. In their daily lives they experience insomnia and digestive problems, lack appetite, sweat easily, show decreased vitality and raised heart rate, and suffer more frequent infections. In the physical realm, they show lower coordination, make more mistakes, even ones that were previously corrected, lack rhythm, have a hard time noticing and correcting technical faults, show a decrease in speed, strength, endurance and reaction time, and are more prone to accidents and injuries.

Psychological symptoms of over-training syndrome

Physical symptoms of overtraining syndrome

Over-training syndrome results from an accumulation of fatigue and stress. Athletes don't get over-training syndrome in a day or even a week; they build up to it over weeks or months of daily acute fatigue with insufficient recovery. If you think you are getting enough recovery time, but you are still feeling over-trained, then you are training too hard. Decrease your training and increase your recovery activities.

It's a short road to over-training. As you train, you experience various types of short-term fatigue, and over time, you get used to it. Meanwhile, school tests, job pressures, big competitions and social events increase the intensity of your work in all areas of life and cut into your recovery time. Rest levels become inadequate. You start using psychological motivation techniques to overcome the strain of fatigue, but it keeps catching up with you. Your nervous system starts to decline in ability and your performance drops. Now your teammates, coaches, family and friends are all urging you to overcome your fatigue and keep performing. It works in the short term: you burn up your last reserve of willpower. Finally you are over-training, and your performance, emotions, and health spiral downward.

The road to overtraining

It is important for every coach to monitor the fatigue level of athletes so that it doesn't accumulate to the over-training stage. It is wise to construct a chart for each athlete to fill out. On the baseline place the days of the month. Down the left side of the page, place various indicators of physical condition: Waking heart rate, length of sleep, quality of sleep, feeling of tiredness during day, interest in training, appetite, ardor to compete, muscle soreness. You might also add space for notes about other indicators—performance on the job, social life, or school grades. Each indicator of physical and mental condition will have five grades on the vertical axis. Five indicates the best condition—no pain, good appetite, high interest in training, peaceful social life, etc., while one is on the bottom and indicates the worst condition—great pain, no appetite, hate training, trauma in social life and so on. Any negative trend in an athlete's physical and psychological indicators should be countered with a lessening of training volume and an examination of rest, recovery and nutrition habits—as well as more personal intervention where needed.

Because of the dangers of overtraining and the frequency with which athletes neglect their basic rest and recovery needs, coaches must teach them and stress them. This is a book about strength training, not about recovery. Nevertheless, here are some key points for a curriculum of rest and recovery education. This list is by no means all-inclusive:

- Sleep habits
- Eating habits, including adequate vitamins
- Rehydration during practice and competition:
- After-practice nutrition
- Mental recovery
- Bodywork, such as massage

Understanding Muscle Soreness

All athletes have experienced soreness after a workout. Soreness comes with training. What most of us don't understand is that most of our post-training soreness comes from chemistry and not from physics. It's not that our muscles are *torn* up by our movements; it is rather that they are *burned* up by the waste products of our metabolism.

Ninety-five percent of your energy production metabolism is very clean. The remaining 5% of your energy production metabolism is very dirty and produces millions of free radicals, very nasty chemicals that act like shrapnel in your body, putting holes in everything they touch. Since you are an athlete and much more active than the average person, your body must go through a greater volume of energy production metabolism. Therefore your body makes a greater amount of free radicals. Tests on animals that were made to exercise in high volume showed that exercise *tripled* the free radical level in their muscles!

After exercise ceases, your body starts a clean up process. Your immune system comes in to clean up the free radical damage. As the neutrophils clean up the cells damaged by exercise-induced free radicals they release masses of free radicals themselves and cause further damage. The result of this unexplainably stupid system is that the athlete feels a two-phase soreness. The first phase comes around 24 hours after exercise as pain from the damage of the original free radicals peaks. The second phase comes 48 hours after exercise as the pain from clean-up induced free radicals peaks. The pain from this second phase can continue for days.

Supplemental antioxidant vitamins can be a great help to athletes. Some studies show that the Recommended Daily Allowance of Vitamin E is only one-fifth of what is needed to deal with everyday free radicals. Since athletes produce possibly 3 times more free radicals than average people their antioxidant requirement could run 10 – 15 times the RDA. So in short, if you are an athlete in training, you must supplement your antioxidants and drink a lot of good water to keep flushing out your system. At the very least you must have supplemental Vitamin E and C.

> *You can overdo supplements too. Consult a physician or nutritionist before starting extensive supplementation.*

2. What is Strength?

What Is Strength in Fencing?

In general, we think of strong guys and girls as being bigger. As a rule of thumb, this has some validity, but not much. If you see a really big muscular guy, you may not want to bet him that you can take his hardest punch in your stomach. But on the other hand, would you bet a little skinny guy that you could take his best shot—after you saw him cleaning up at a karate tournament? Would you bet a 115-pound figure skater that you could do a one-legged step-up with more weight on your back than she could? The lightweight karate practitioner has a lot of *power* in his small-diameter arms. The dainty figure skater has *explosive strength* in her legs.

There are different ways of expressing strength. Power lifters balance and raise hundreds of pounds, but just once, and they can take all the time they need. Marathoners pound the pavement with their own bodyweight thousands and thousands of times. Figure skaters balance, turn, and launch their body into the air while sliding over the ice. Karate practitioners project many pounds of force through two knuckles in a fraction of a second. Basketball players accelerate into a full sprint, then stop in an instant. Each of these endeavors requires its own unique type of strength. Each athlete is strong in his or her own way, though some are considered dainty and others burly.

From these examples we can derive a checklist to discover the parameters of strength in any given sport, then see what's needed for fencing.

- How much force is needed in your sport? Football linemen deliver extremely heavy forces; ping-pong players deliver extremely light blows.
  In fencing, the forces we need to apply are not very great compared to the forces in some other sports. *Force*
- How much time do you have to deliver the force needed in your sport? A power lifter may lift the weight very slowly, while a counterpunching boxer has only a split second in which to throw his punch before the opponent's attack lands.
  Fencers have very little time—often only a fraction of a second—to deliver their hit. *Time*
- How often—and for how long—are the forces in your sport required? Marathoners must propel their bodyweight steadily forward over two hours, whereas long jumpers must propel their bodyweight forward for a very short time once or twice every 15 minutes.
  The forces required in fencing must be applied over and over again, but only for three minutes followed by a rest period. Maximum effort is applied for periods that rarely reach as much as thirty seconds. *Frequency and duration*
- How much acceleration is required? A fast sport may not have extreme acceleration. For example a baseball pitcher's hand may be moving at 100 mph at the moment of release, but that speed requires a relatively lengthy wind-up.
  In fencing, extreme acceleration is often necessary—for example, when a lunge or fleche begins from a standing start or when the final movement of an attack must catch a retreating opponent. *Acceleration*
- How much deceleration is necessary? A sprinter runs in one direction only and coasts to a stop at the end of a race. But rapid

Deceleration

deceleration is more difficult than rapid acceleration. Think of a major league baseball player trying to stop his swing at a bad pitch.

Fencing requires frequent whole-body deceleration. A fencer must be able to move backward, quickly stop to parry, and go forward quickly to riposte.

Arm deceleration is also very important in martial arts like boxing or fencing: the athlete's arm must recover from a missed attempt and prepare for the next action.

- How much balance is needed in your sport in order for your strength to be expressed? What are the balancing components of the strength expression in your sport? Many things can challenge our balance in sports:

Balance

  - Angles of force (Think of a soccer player trying to kick the ball sideways while running forward)
    In fencing, the arm movements require a variety of angles. The legs and feet require fewer angles, but they are specialized.

  - Collision impact (Think of a check in hockey or a block in football,)
    The fencer must be prepared for occasional, minor collision impact.

  - Foot slippage (Think of skating or skiing)
    In fencing, foot slippage is (usually) limited.

  - Quick starts, stops, and changes of direction (Think of a basketball player running, stopping, faking, yet maintaining balance to make an accurate shot.)
    In fencing, there are constant quick starts and stops.

Understand the strength require-ments of fencing

Figuring out these strength requirements for fencers is our first step toward an intelligent approach to training for success. It gives us a way to compare fencing to other sports, to think of ourselves as part of the sports pantheon. What kind of football player would make the best fencer—an offensive lineman, a cornerback, or a wide-out? What track and field events would make a good cross-training program for a fencer? What sport is most like fencing from an athletic point of view—baseball, basketball, karate, or figure skating? These three questions make good topics for team discussion; they also have practical uses such as cross train-ing, filling out a team with athletes from other sports, and knowing which sports to observe in order to pick up new ideas, techniques and inspiration.

In addition, knowing fencing's strength requirements gives us an idea of what kind of strength we need and what kind we don't. For example, jogging (or anything slow) should not be the final stage of a fencing conditioning program. Fencers need speed. Fencers may do slow weightlifting and slow running for the sake of toughness, but they must transform this toughness into speed by using other, faster training exercises. And since fencers need starting and stopping abil-ity, they may begin with stationary weightlifting and unidirectional running, but they must eventually progress by means of ballistic and multidirectional workouts in the final stages of a strength training program.

3. What Makes a Strong Muscle?

The types of strength necessary for success in fencing have a physiological foundation. As a response to training, the body rebuilds and improves itself. It rebuilds muscle cells, nerve tissue, connective tissue, circulatory tissue, and cell components that produce energy. These physiological changes are the foundation of all later work, both in strength training and in development of sports skills. Athletes must have solid and extensive muscle, nervous, connective, circulatory, and energy systems before they can perform advanced exercises or sports skills with any kind of proficiency.

Through strength training, the athlete also develops skills. Skills contribute to all strength training exercises. Some exercises make greater demands on skill but no exercise is completely devoid of a skill component.

Here is a survey of the changes that come from basic strength training. Some of them are physiological changes and some of them are skills.

Does Strength Mean Bigger Muscles?

When we get stronger, do we really get bigger? Often, yes. But weight and size don't always equate with strength. Kim Goss, a noted writer on strength training, and former strength coach at the Air Force Academy, likes to tell the story of the time his college basketball players were working on one-legged step-ups with barbells across their backs. Coach Goss thought that they were doing it lazily, so he called on one of his figure skaters, who was standing nearby. He asked her to demonstrate the exercise. This 115-pound woman proceeded to do step-ups with 250 pounds on her back, more than the weight that any of the big basketball players could handle. The basketball team slunk home that day.

Sometimes the muscle does get bigger. After the athlete works through a strength-training program, the muscle holds more fuel. It contains more contractile proteins (the little chemical machines that make a muscle pull.) It contains more supportive connective tissue. It contains more blood vessels. It is larger in cross-sectional area but more importantly, it is also *healthier* in many ways. It is not simply large.

If big and bulky is not our natural size, then getting big and bulky is very unlikely. Natural bodybuilders go through extreme regimens of vitamin intake, food intake, rest and workouts to get their extreme size. And many large athletes have resorted to unnatural, illegal chemical means in their quest to get big. Fortunately, as we've seen, fencers don't have to go that far. A fencer's muscles may get bigger, but the size that comes from natural strength training is the result of developing a healthy muscle.

Fencers shouldn't hope that their strength training will give them the physiques of bodybuilders. On the other hand, they need not worry that strength training will make them bulky and slow. Through strength training the fencer will maximize his or her strength potential by developing healthy muscles with the following characteristics

Characteristics of healthy muscles

1. Increased Neural Drive

The largest part of the strength gains from a strength training program comes from *increased neural drive*. A novice may only be able to recruit 60% of the mass of a muscle—in other words, even at maximum effort, 40% of a novice athlete's muscle cells are resting. With training, the athlete may learn to call upon 85% of muscle mass. The nerves become more active and coordinated and the athlete's functional strength increases, even within the first 2 or 3 weeks of the program. Conversely, through disuse, an athlete's nerves become less active, and less and less muscle mass is stimulated into action.

Think about how a muscle operates—the biceps, for example. We use the biceps to flex the arm at the elbow. We use the same muscle to pick up a 60-pound bag of cement, swing a 14-pound bowling ball, and to pick up a one-ounce fork loaded with a half ounce of egg and gently place it in our mouth. How do we modify the strength for each task? By the amount of nerve energy, biological electricity so to speak, we put into the muscle.

The muscle is made of small motor units, each consisting of one nerve supplying a certain number of muscle cells. Each motor unit is either on or off. There is no such thing as halfway on. Some motor units contract when the electrical signal is low, some when it is medium, and some when it is high. The ones that contract with a low impulse will also contract when the nerve signal is medium or high. Some parts of the muscle never contract except in a dire emergency. To use a fork at the table, we put out a low signal and get a gentle action. But to use a fork as a weapon, the athlete needs a powerful signal from the nervous system.

Training optimizes performance in the following ways:

How training improves performance

- It teaches the *nervous system*
  - to call upon more of the available muscle fibers
  - to call upon all parts of the muscle at the same time (rather than a flickering, uncoordinated cell recruitment).
- It teaches *all of the muscles needed*
  - to fire at the correct time.
- It teaches the *athlete*
  - to recruit the muscle fibers quickly.
  - to send more electrical energy to the muscles.

So far, so good. But training and competition put a strain on nerve cells. After a short period of maximum work, the nerve cell goes into a state of inhibition to protect itself from overwork. In the state of inhibition, the nerve cell will not activate as it usually does, no matter how hard the athlete tries. Physical force and coordination decline quickly. An experiment with a 30-second maximum-intensity contraction has shown that, by the end of the 30-second time period, nerve cells had reduced their firing frequency by 80%. Hence, after becoming tired, especially when learning a new skill, the athlete must get enough rest to allow the nerves to recover their full capacity. Otherwise, the athlete is learning with a semi-functional nervous system.

2. Increased Skill and Coordination

An athlete can't *express* strength without skill and coordination. All the parts within one muscle must learn to contract in unison. All the muscles that make up a larger movement must work together. Some move the arm, some stabilize the joints and other parts of the body, and some decelerate the limb after it moves. In complete bodily motions such as the fencing lunge, or the weightlifting lunge, squat or clean, almost every bone, muscle and sinew of the body must be in the right place doing the right job at the right time to get maximum force production. Strength training is a highly skilled task.

Physical therapists use the term "motor engram," from "motor," meaning pertaining to movement, and "engram," meaning a lasting mark or trace. The term *engram* applies to the bioelectrical trace associated with storing a memory in the nervous system. Muscles have memory. A *motor engram* is a memory that resides *in the muscles*. When an athlete makes a particular movement, an electrical message passes through some of the numerous nerve passages in their body, firing off the correct muscles with proper coordination and force.

Motor engrams

If the athlete *repeats* that movement, the resistance in that unique electrical pathway *decreases*—it gets easier for the message to pass. If the athlete tries to change the movement, the brain will try to send a message down a different pathway. But the message will often slide down the old, low resistance path and produce the old movement. The old movement will take a great effort to unlearn. That's why it is best for the athlete to learn any movement the right way the first time. It takes less than three hundred tries to learn a movement, but if it's learned the wrong way it takes three *thousand* tries to re-learn it the right way.

A quality motor engram is made by repetition that has three qualities: *accuracy, consistency*, and *real speed*. When athletes execute repetitions of their strength training exercises, they should start with a movement that is accurate, repeat it consistently, and then bring it up to speed.

Accuracy, consistency, and real speed make quality motor engrams

The strength training described in this book, when done correctly, creates a more highly skilled body. The athlete's body learns every aspect of strength: balance, acceleration, deceleration, ability to change direction, and so on. These are all basic bodily skills. Once the body is skilled, the fencer and the coach work together to make the skilled body do fencing.

This idea of the engram, the complicated physical pathway that burns itself into the body, is essential to understanding the effect of strength training on the development of athletic skill. When athletes do an exercise, they stand a certain way, they hold their head a certain way, they clench their jaw a certain way. If that way is a bad way for fencing in a bout, then the athlete is learning a bad habit, a negative skill. The athlete and the coach can use strength training exercises to erase bodily habits that are hurting the fencer's success or to begin bodily habits that will lead to good fencing moves.

3. Balanced Progress Makes Stronger Connective Tissue

All movement is accomplished by muscle contraction; that is, the muscle pulls inward on the bones or tissue it is attached to. Despite the name, the muscles don't actually get shorter in every case: when we lower a weight slowly, the muscles actually lengthen while pulling inward. The kind of contraction where the muscle actually gets shorter is called *concentric contraction,* while the kind where the muscle lengthens is called *eccentric contraction.*

Muscle contraction: Concentric means the muscle gets shorter. Eccentric means the muscle gets longer

Muscles develop an increased and more efficient ability to contract in reaction to the stresses of strength training. This increased ability to contract begins in a matter of days: that is why people feel stronger during the first week or two of a lifting program. It's not that the muscles have gotten bigger or stronger; they've just gotten more coordinated. If athletes try to vault forward off these strength gains and lift more and more heavily over the third through sixth weeks of their training, they will likely experience severe muscle and joint soreness that may retard their training for the next few weeks or months.

This drop-off in strength gains and increase in pain can be explained by the fact that connective tissue (muscle sheaths, tendons, ligaments and joint capsules) and harder tissue such as bone and cartilage take weeks and even months of training to develop. Connective tissue takes 5 – 7 times longer to develop. All these connective tissue improvements contribute to the functional improvement of the athlete. They make their body better able to resist injury and handle the dynamic situations of athletic performance. In addition, they add to the size of the muscle.

Don't rush your training! Connective tissue takes 5 – 7 times longer to develop than muscle.

Hence, if you are a strength-training novice, or you've taken a long time off from training, or you're simply new to sports, you have to go at your training program slowly. Athletes should not progress to heavier weights or ballistic training (plyometrics) until their connective tissue has caught up with their muscular strength.

The time between your initial strength gains and the moment when your connective tissue has caught up to these strength gains is a lag time. To prevent boredom and general waste of time during that lag period, your strength training program can work on your nervous system by challenging your skill and balance instead of your raw strength. And you can certainly mix in easy plyometric movements such as the Dot Drill (p. 130) to promote speed. (I'll explain these terms later.)

Running builds tough connective tissue.

Simple running has been shown to toughen the connective tissue in the legs. Some studies suggest that faster running is more effective for connective tissue development. When running, it is not necessary to run continuously without resting. Run shorter distances such as miles, half-miles and quarter-miles. Run at a speed where you "feel the burn." Then take a rest and run again until you've logged your target distance. This is more effective at toughening connective tissue than long, continuous runs. I usually have my high school fencers run fast quarter miles—with rest periods in between.

The days when a fencer trained only by fencing are long gone!

If fencing is such a special sport, why not just fence instead of running and strength training? The days when a fencer's training consisted in simply fencing three days a week are long gone. Every high-level sports program, including figure skating, now includes a strength training component. Only a few "naturals" can achieve high results by fencing alone—and they would probably get better results by adding other kinds of training.

Strengthening connective tissue can also influence the apparent strength of an athlete. The body has special sensors on the tendons of every joint that monitor the stress that the tendon is under. When the tendon comes near the breaking point, the body cuts off the electrical energy to the muscle and reduces its ability to contract. This feedback happens in a split second, so it seems to the observer as though the muscle is weak. In fact, the body has temporarily reduced the strength ability of the muscle so it won't tear other parts of the body asunder. This protective mechanism can be overcome in an emergency, but it is not a good idea under most other circumstances.

This protective mechanism gives an additional insight into apparent weakness. Suppose an athlete is trying to do an exercise or a skill but appears to be too weak to do it well. There are two possible explanations:

- The muscles are in fact simply too weak, or
- The connective tissue or the stabilizer muscles are too weak, so that the athlete's body is shutting down the major muscles so they don't rip themselves apart.

Since the coach doesn't know for sure why the weakness is occurring, he or she should start that athlete's strength training program from the ground up, first challenging connective tissue (with body-weight or lightly-weighted exercises) and only then progressing to exercises and weights that challenge the major muscles. Later, I will describe this progression in more detail.

4. Increased Blood Supply

The body is capable of building new capillaries to supply blood to areas where there is a special need for oxygen and nutrients. When there is chronic demand for increased blood supply, which is to say when there is chronic exercise, the body will increase the number of supply routes. (This same ability is used insidiously by cancer cells. They lodge somewhere in the body then send out the chemical signals that cause the body to build supply routes to them, thus nourishing their harmful growth. Learning how to shut off these destructive signals is one of the interesting areas of cancer research. But I digress.)

5. Energy System Improvements

As Fred Hatfield says, every creature from a bear to a butterfly uses the same cellular energy, the stuff called adenosine triphosphate or ATP. This energy fuels the cellular machinery that gives the bear the ability to tear the bark off of a tree and the butterfly the ability to migrate its paper-light body a thousand miles on the wing.

When most of us think of having a lot of energy, we are thinking of the ability to keep going hour after hour and sometimes day after day. This way of thinking is accurate—up to a point. To keep going does not mean the same thing to a fencer as it does to a marathoner or a gymnast. Each athlete must keep going at a different sort of thing. The marathoner must keep the stride going very quickly for hours. The gymnast working on the rings must support his body weight on his arms for minutes. Fencers must be able to advance and retreat continuously for perhaps a dozen seconds (more in epee, less in sabre), move explosively for a few steps, scream at the top of their lungs and pump their fist repeatedly, rest briefly, and then repeat the process continuously for up to three minutes (we could do without the screaming)—all while remaining fully alert and even splitting their concentration in several directions. These are completely different types of endurance.

There is more to endurance than improved functioning of cardiopulmonary capacity. The body does need a good distribution of blood supply to provide the muscles with their metabolic needs. But muscles themselves respond to training of *all kinds*. This includes strength training, a type of training not normally associated with endurance. The muscles do this by improving their energy systems. In general terms, the muscles improve their ability to quickly manufacture and burn their fuel, ATP. This is called local muscular endurance.

The endurance equation has two parts: cardiopulmonary endurance and local muscular endurance. Another way of thinking of it is that the body has two energy systems: one slow—the cardiopulmonary system, which drives the aerobic energy system, and one fast, made up of the lactic acid and anaerobic pathways. The slow energy system refuels the fast energy system during every break in the action and in the longer rests between bouts. The fast energy system fuels quick movement

Endurance works through two energy systems: one fast and one slow. The fast system includes the lactic acid and anaerobic pathways. The slow system is the aerobic system.

directly and can be virtually exhausted after only three straight minutes of hard, quick exercise.

Exercise of specific muscles improves local muscular endurance more with than does general aerobic training, which only asks the legs to move parallel to each other and straight ahead. Fencers need the muscle-specific endurance that comes from strength training *in addition to* the cardiopulmonary endurance that comes from running.

Some explosive sport athletes try to get away with very little cardiopulmonary training. But this is not always wise. The increased oxygen-transfer capacity that comes from long-distance endurance training helps fencers to recover their explosive ability over a shorter rest period. An athlete with improved cardio endurance will be stronger from bout to bout and from stage to stage in a 15-touch bout or a continuous team match.

Cardio endurance means quicker recovery.

In summary, there are two necessary parts to energy system training: cardiopulmonary base training and local muscular endurance training. Cardiopulmonary ability provides the base for all human activity from reading or writing to running. In fencing, cardiopulmonary machinery is the base, the foundation, of local muscular endurance. If your joints are temporarily too beat up to get out and pound the pavement with a running program, you can still work your cardiopulmonary base (perhaps I should say you *must* work your cardiopulmonary base) on the treadmill or the stationary bike at a speed which demands your target heart rate.

And then, building on the cardiopulmonary base, strength training produces local muscular endurance.

3. Progressive Overload:

Making the Workout Harder So You Get Stronger

This chapter discusses the nature of each of the stimuli that athletes must present to their bodies to encourage them to grow strong. The coach and athlete must understand the nature of the stimuli in order to grasp the logic of the program as a whole and thus to develop a flexible program to suit individual needs. This chapter is a list of the important stimuli that the body responds to and how it responds to them by getting stronger.

In the old days, an athlete got progressively stronger by lifting progressively more weight—more weight on each repetition, more repetitions of a particular weight in a set, and more sets of repetitions. But there is much more to successful strength training than lifting more weight more times. This chapter will help you understand the difference.

The central concept here is *progressive overload.* When you overload your body you cause one of two things: adaptation or breakdown. The purpose of strength training is to get the body to adapt, rather than break down. The athlete's body *needs* overload; it needs a "reason" to grow, which means it needs to be taxed. Without this stressful stimulation, it will in a sense become "uninterested" in strength, level off in its development, or even become weaker. On the other hand, if the athlete increases the load too rapidly, the body will in a sense get "discouraged" and stop trying to get stronger. So, progressive overload is not the same as constant overload. Don't overload all the time!

When you overload your body, it either adapts or breaks down. In strength training, we want it to adapt.

The most basic plan is to work one overload session a week. Between overloading sessions, the athlete should work easier sessions where their body is not overloaded and has a chance to recover. *This principle applies in all training sessions,* whether they are predominantly skill-oriented, strength-oriented, or a mixture of the two. As we shall see, these alternating cycles of harder and easier work make the athlete's body overcompensate and get a little stronger than it needs to be.

Maintaining Form and Posture

Posture and exercise form should be excellent every day, not just on one overload day per week. Good exercise form and posture must be learned just like any other skill. Once the athlete can execute each exercise with good form and posture, *the loss of good form becomes the measure of fatigue.* Form and posture should be perfect and automatic. Cease repetitions of the exercise when your form fails, rest, and then, if necessary, do another set *with good form.*

Maintaining posture is the first rule of good strength training. The most critical thing people learn from strength training is their ideal power position. When you do resistance exercises over and over, you are learning, in a lasting, unconscious way, a posture where you feel powerful. You will resort to this position under stress—even if it is an anatomically disadvantageous position in which your energy will be wasted and body parts will rub against each other and wear out. Through exercise, you must teach your body the *truly* most powerful position from which to act, which is good posture. When you do powerful strength training exercises from this position, it will burn it into your brain: "*Here* is where I am most powerful." And you will learn to use these most anatomically advantageous positions in sports competition as well as in the rest of your life.

Stop the exercise when you can no longer maintain good form and posture.

Weight and Percentage of 1 Rep Max (1RM)

Strength trainers use the measure of the one-repetition maximum, known as 1 Rep Max or 1RM as a gauge of personal strength and an indicator of relative progress in strength training. Your 1RM is the amount of weight you can lift just once in a given exercise *before your form begins to degrade* on your next attempt. We are *not* talking about total muscle failure here. The 1RM is the heaviest amount you can lift once *with correct form*.

Don't risk injury by lifting a huge weight to determine your 1RM–you can *extrapolate* your 1RM instead. If you exercise with a lower weight until your form degrades, you can use the chart below to determine the maximum number of reps you can do with that weight. Find that number of reps on the following table (condensed from Poliquin) to find what percentage of 1RM that weight is and thus estimate the 1RM. In addition, you can use the table to discover the training effect of each number of reps.

Table 1: The Relationship of Reps, Weight and Their Associated Training Effects

Choose the number of reps in a set according to the training effect you're after.

Number of Repetitions to fatigue (loss of form):	3 reps	7 reps	12 reps	20 reps
Associated percentage of 1RM:	90% of 1RM	80% of 1RM	70% of 1RM	60% of 1RM
Primary training effect of a set with this number of repetitions:	Improved neural and endocrine drive	Compromise between strength and drive	Maximal strength, greater size	Improved local strength endurance

Let's take a moment to define the three major training effects listed on the last row of Table 1. Reading from right to left:

Local strength endurance

- *Local strength endurance* has a toughening effect. With solid 20-rep sets, the body improves coordination, energy, blood supply and connective tissue, all preparing for more strenuous activities.

Maximal strength development

- *Maximal strength development* is a building phase. All the parts listed in strength endurance continue to improve with maximal strength sets. Also, if the muscles have the ability to get bigger, 12-rep sets have the greatest chance of bringing out this ability.

Neural and endocrine drive

- *Neural and endocrine drive* are the body's ability to produce the most explosive use of strength. With an increase in neural drive it is as though the body is sending a louder bioelectric call to the muscles and therefore recruiting more cells and recruiting them in a more perfectly coordinated manner. With an increase in endocrine drive it is as though the body is more excited and more focused and therefore better prepared to deal with the stress of a great effort and better prepared to perform a "superhuman" feat.

In Table 1, each percentage of 1RM is a relative weight used to control the effect of the exercise. For each athlete it is the actual number of pounds that produces a set ending in fatigue after the given number of repetitions in order to achieve the desired effect. Thus, once you learn your own strength, you should choose a weight that causes fatigue within the desired number of reps, thus producing the desired training effect.

1RM is a theoretical number. When you enter the world of strength training you will almost inevitably hear about 1RM and percentage of 1RM. It's like being in medicine and hearing the Latin names for illnesses. You quickly learn that "tonsillitis" is just another way of saying "sick tonsils." Similarly, 70% 1RM is just another way of saying "For this exercise set use a weight that will tire you out in 12 reps." (We get this translation of percentage of 1RM into repetitions from the chart above.) Personally, I don't use percentage of 1RM when talking to athletes. I just talk about number of reps and the training effect.

Athletes vary in their abilities from day to day. One day they have gone up a little in ability, another day they have gone down a little. The purpose of tracking the number of reps and percentage of 1RM is to control the effect of the exercise as much as is humanly possible. It's not necessary to get obsessed and carry a calculator around the training room. The most important method of controlling a workout is to keep track of what gets accomplished in each workout. For each exercise in each workout, write down exercises, weight, reps, sets and other variables. Try to get the number of reps as close as possible to your training objective.

And keep a record! Writing it down also helps you see if you are getting stronger. Can you do more reps this week than you did two or three weeks ago? Can you do more weight this week than you did two or three weeks ago? Is it easier to do the same number of reps and the same weight you did last week? If the answer to any of these is yes then you are improving. Your body is learning and adapting.

Keep a record of your workouts.

When you pick up a weight and begin a certain exercise, how do you know when you will fatigue? You can probably figure this out from the written history of your recent workouts. If you don't have much of a workout history, however, or if you are having a day when you are stronger or weaker than you have been in the past, you may not know how much weight you should put on the bar to get a desired training effect. So it is not uncommon that the first set in a workout is too heavy or too light to produce the desired training effect. In that case, simply put the bar down, take a rest period and adjust the weight appropriately for the next set.

Here's how to use the table. If you just did seven good repetitions of the military press at 40 pounds, the table predicts that your one-rep max will be fifty pounds and the effect of seven reps will be a balance between drive and strength. If you want to concentrate on neural and endocrine drive alone, increase the weight to forty-five pounds and do only three reps. If you want to maximize strength, drop the weight to thirty-five pounds and work 12-rep sets. And if you are trying to maximize endurance, you would do 20-rep sets at only thirty pounds.

Athletes with different levels of experience benefit from working different areas of the rep/weight table. Novices will benefit from 40-60% 1RM during the first eight sessions. As the table indicates, this builds local strength endurance. 40-60% 1RM means working more than 20 repetitions. After those first eight sessions, the athlete graduates from novice to beginner and should spend the remainder of the first year of training in the 60-70% range, perhaps around fifteen reps, building strength as well as endurance.

There is so much for the body to learn in this first cycle of lifting that there is no need to challenge it with the greater weights. First groove the form and build the neural coordination, energy systems, blood vessels, and connective tissue strength. Only then should you attempt to lift heavily and amplify the neural drive.

After a certain amount of time, athletes, especially beginners, will push their 1RM up because they are now actually stronger, even though they have only lifted

After a while, stop increasing 1RM and progress to stability, coordination, and speed.

with 40 – 70% of their 1RM. So, 70% 1RM — the weight where they can do 12 good reps — will gradually become a higher actual weight over the course of one or two months of training. But after a certain point *the athlete should stop trying to push the 1RM up* and begin to add other forms of overload to their workout. At this point, athletes should begin to work on stability, coordination and speed as outlined in more detail below.

After the first *year* of training, the athlete should choose his or her workout according to the needs of his or her sport. Explosive sports like fencing require most of the training time to be in the low part of the 60 – 90% training range. For fencers who are experienced weight trainers, the mixture of endurance sets, strength sets, and drive sets will look like the pyramid in Table 2.

The base of the pyramid represents *local muscular endurance* development: the largest number of training days are spent doing sets in the neighborhood of 12 – 20 reps for maximal local muscular endurance development. The middle of the pyramid represents *strength* development: a medium number of training days are spent doing 7 – 12 rep sets for a compromise of strength and drive. The top of the pyramid is *drive* development: a small number of training days are spent doing 3 – 7 rep sets for neural and endocrine drive.

Time Under Tension, Speed of Repetition, and Number of Sets

The body gets stronger in response to *time under tension* — the basic stimulus that causes the body to compensate by producing more strength.

Each set produces a certain amount of time under tension, defined as the time it takes to do both the concentric and eccentric portions of a repetition multiplied by the number of repetitions in a set. The muscles should be under tension for *at most 60 seconds per set*, or nervous system and energy system fatigue will make the muscles sluggish and retard the effect of the exercise. For example, when doing a bench press set of 20 repetitions, an athlete can spend one second on each up

Table 2: Training Goals in Relation to Number of Training Days

DRIVE
1 Workout per Cycle

STRENGTH
2 Workouts per Cycle

MUSCULAR ENDURANCE
3 Workouts per Cycle

stroke and do each down stroke with a 2-second cadence for a total of 60 seconds under tension. (When an athlete is doing the novice routine of greater than 20 reps it might be difficult to keep the set under 60 seconds. But this is OK at this stage.)

Athletes should not think of 20-rep sets as "baby work" simply because beginners do them too or because they aren't "allowed" to hoist the hefty weights that would increase their stud factor. For fencers and other martial artists, repetitive movement of lighter weights is what they do in competition. They must have strength endurance for their sport. *And an important way to train for strength endurance is 20-rep sets!*

On the other hand, fencers should not think of power sets as something only for football players and other big athletes. The neural drive that develops from heavy sets can be helpful for development of explosiveness (think of a lunge or fleche!). If world-class figure skaters can benefit from 1 – 3-rep sets—and they can—then so can fencers!

> - ***Athletes should have at least one year of quality weight training and strong and alert spotters before executing heavy sets.***
> - ***The athlete or the coach should call off the heavy sets if there is any indication that the athlete is fatigued from previous workouts or showing signs of substandard performance.***
> - ***An athlete must be at his or her best when attempting heavy weights, not using guts and willpower to get through a tough time.***

If an athlete chooses to execute a set for the purpose of developing neural drive, it is easy to see that lifting a set of 3 or fewer reps will produce very little time under tension if the repetitions are not done very slowly. *Very slow reps of up to 10 seconds each* are quite valuable for a less experienced lifter and for the first few weeks of an advanced lifter's program.

Sooner or later, the athlete will advance to repetitions at maximum speed. Maximum speed with a heavier weight is relatively slow, but it is nevertheless maximum speed because the athlete pushes hard all the way through the lift, thus getting maximum neural drive. Maximum speed combined with low reps, however, will result in low time under tension. In order to achieve adequate time under tension, the athlete should do more low-rep sets.

The approximate range of the ratio of reps to sets is, on the high end, 15 sets of one repetition of 100% 1RM and, on the low end, 2 sets of 20-plus repetitions with 40 – 60% 1RM. *Be sure to allow for adequate rest time between sets!* (See the next section.)

Early in training, 1 – 2 sets of each exercise will produce neural improvement and strength gains. Later, 3 – 6 sets of each exercise will work other physical aspects of the muscle. Increase sets and number of workouts only when you stop gaining in strength. At that point, gradually increase the amount of work, doing the least work in order to accomplish improvement. Two sessions per week will be adequate at first. Gradually increase the workload from there.

Limit the duration of the workout. A total of 20 – 25 sets at one session is ideal. The maximum number of sets in a single session should be 30 – 35. Otherwise, neural fatigue will ruin the effect of the work. If you need more work, rest an hour; then resume.

If you are feeling tired on a given day, do fewer sets but maintain the tension. It is recommended to decrease time rather than tension.

Work versus Rest Period

For explosive sports such as fencing, the normal rest period between sets of strength-training exercises should be anywhere from 3 – 5 minutes. This allows for total recovery. Total recovery allows for the maximum strength effect of the exercises on the muscles. This routine is not intended to copy the rest/work conditions of a fencing bout. These produce more "heavy breathing," and this heavy breathing is not an ideal metabolic condition in which to develop strong muscles.

Greater intensity demands more rest!

Greater intensity—produced by an increase in weight, speed or skill— requires more rest. If the ability to do the skill is deteriorating between sets, consider increasing the rest time. On the other hand, most experts believe that rest periods greater than seven minutes allow the body to cool down too much and therefore increase the risk of injury. Therefore, if the athlete seems to need seven minutes or more to recover the ability to do a certain skill, the rest period should include activity such as walking. During normal rest periods, athletes can practice breathing exercises which can later be used to enhance their mental calm and physical recovery during breaks in competition.

Stability/Instability

Every athlete can do more weight in a given exercise on a weight machine like those we see in health clubs. This has the least instability. There's more instability with a barbell, and more still with dumbbells, and still more when we introduce an exercise ball or a soft mat. Someone who is new to weightlifting may be introduced to the practice by working on a machine to build self-confidence. Then he or she may advance to a barbell. At this point, *they must reduce the weight used* because the barbell is less stable and will tax their stabilizer muscles. Later they can advance to dumbbells, which are less stable than the barbell and require another decrease in weight.

When first increasing instability, decrease the resistance!

Despite the reduction in resistance, dumbbells are more functional because they teach the athlete to control the force in every direction. The athlete must learn to stabilize the weight. This is like real life: in competition, athletes will not be pushing weights in a track. They will face a dynamic and unstable situation, plus an opponent who is trying to trick them into failure.

Thus, after developing basic form and strength with basic weightlifting exercises, athletes can add increasing instability to their strength training program.

> *Instability decreases the amount of weight an athlete can handle. When instability increases, weight must decrease until the athlete demonstrates increased stabilizer strength and nerve coordination and can safely and surely handle more weight. Increase weight slowly.*

Here are some basic ways to increase instability, using the bench press as an example

1. Progress from a barbell to dumbbells.
2. Progress from synchronized dumbbells to alternating dumbbells.
3. Progress from 2 dumbbells to a one-armed single dumbbell exercise.
4. Progress from lying or sitting on a bench to lying squarely on a Swiss ball. Move from lying squarely on a Swiss ball to lying off-center on a Swiss ball.
5. Progress from lying to a standing cable push on two legs.

6. Progress from a basic standing cable push to a cable push done standing on one leg opposite the pushing hand.
7. Progress to standing on one leg on the same side as the pushing hand.

The alternating and single arm dumbbell exercises are widely considered to be superior to barbell exercises for athletes whose sport requires the use of one arm at a time, such as fencing or throwing. It is quite likely that this is a neurological effect—that the body learns in this way how to best perform a one-sided operation.

Alternating-arm dumbbell exercises and single-arm dumbbell exercises are more effective training tools in sports that use one arm at a time —like fencing!

Nevertheless, *fencers can begin their training with barbells* for the purpose of developing basic strength and basic weight training abilities. Some exercises, such as the power clean, will always be done with a barbell because it is a *whole body explosion exercise*, not particularly a limb-strengthening exercise.

Skill Complexity

As the skill necessary to complete the exercise increases, then the intensity of the exercise increases. Studies have shown that athletes exposed to increased skill demands exhibit increased heart rate even though the pace and weight of the exercise remains the same. It seems that increased concentration by itself makes more sweat and a faster heart beat.

The application to fencing seems obvious. The fencer may know the beat, parry, thrust, advance, retreat and lunge and have practiced each one many times over. But when presented with a challenging combination of movements with varying cues and responses, the same moves become more physically taxing. *This skill complexity effect occurs also in strength training exercises.*

More complex skills are physically more demanding.

For example, suppose you have been working the basic bench press and its variations. You have advanced, step by step (see above) from a barbell bench press to one-arm dumbbell bench presses. For the next advance, you want to do the same exercise on your feet, in the form of a cable push. It might seem that this is simply the same exercise, only vertical. But previously, when you pushed on the weight, you were supported and stabilized by the bench. Standing up, you have to stabilize yourself as you push. In fact, the standing cable push is much more complex than anything done before: it is a coordinated combination involving the legs, abs, and arms in a new and neurologically complex skill. You will need to scale down the weight until you have mastered the skill! Wherever complexity is added weight should be reduced until the athlete has proven the ability to execute with perfect form.

At the beginning of a complex skill, the coach should inspect the athlete from head to toe to be sure posture and form are correct. The athlete should reduce the weight until the form is perfect and automatic. The same holds for totally new exercises, such as plyometric jumping and throwing. Start with low intensity, which means slow speed and light weight, until the form and posture is perfect and automatic.

Speed of Movement

In a well-known experiment, athletes performed a weighted squat while standing on a plate that measured the force going through their feet and into the ground—first when the athlete lifted the weight in 1.5 seconds, then when the same athlete lifted the same weight in 0.75 seconds. The faster lift took half the time. But the measurement on the plate showed that the lift put *four times* the force through the athlete's feet and into the ground. *If an athlete lifts twice as fast, the force quadruples* through the feet, the spine and every other part of the body below the weight.

*Work on the speed
of your strength.*

Speed is essential to sports performance. In most sports, just bringing a large amount of force to bear on an object or opponent is not enough. (This is obviously true in fencing.) The athlete must be able to bring that force to bear quickly. Except for sports in which speed is not an issue, like power lifting, athletes need to work on the speed of their strength. Once physically prepared, they must add speed to a workout and know how to modify a workout to deal wisely with the exponentially increased forces. The application to fencing should also be obvious.

When you start adding speed to a workout, start by reducing the weight to 25% of what you can normally handle. For example, an athlete beginning plyometrics has to deal with *two* new overload variables, speed and complexity. So, when starting heavy plyometrics such as medicine balls and box jumps (to be covered later), act as if you were starting the strength training program over again: go light and concentrate on good form and posture.

Deceleration

Deceleration is harder on the body than acceleration. There are two sorts of deceleration.

Slow Deceleration

First, there is the simple, slow-speed act of lowering a weight. This occurs during any weightlifting action where the muscle is elongating while at the same time trying to contract in an effort to keep the weight from crashing down with increasing speed. The muscle is slowing this acceleration. In the bench press, this would be the act of lowering the bar to the chest. This phase of the lift is called the "negative" or "eccentric" portion of the lift, with the muscle-shortening contraction being the "positive" or "concentric" portion of the lift. *The eccentric portion of the lift is more stressful and causes more muscle soreness than the concentric.*

The lowering part of any lift is the hardest and produces the most muscle soreness in the two days after a workout. *Novices and beginners should de-emphasize the eccentric portion of the lift in terms of its proportion of the time under tension in order to reduce the pain of their introduction to strength training.* So if the concentric (lifting) phase of the motion is done to a 3 or 4 count the eccentric (lowering) phase should be done with a 1 or 2 count. This doesn't mean that the athlete should let the bar slam down on their chest in order to de-emphasize the eccentric portion of the bench press. Simply decrease the eccentric time under tension in a safe way.

Rapid Deceleration

*Take care with the
deceleration phase of
your exercise.*

For the explosive speed athlete, on the other hand, deceleration is one of the most valuable parts of strength training. This is especially true for martial artists, such as fencers and boxers. Very often, the fastest athlete is the one who can *stop* the explosive action most effectively. If a fencer has muscles strong enough to stop a series of rapid advances and reverse direction, he or she can go forward at full speed without fear of tearing apart or running into the opponent's point in line. That fencer's body knows, from the inside, whether a certain forward speed is dangerous. The stronger the fencer is, the faster his body will let him go.

When you are doing an action like swinging a bat, jumping down from a box, or playing catch with a heavy ball, the negative portion puts the most stress on the body. *Stopping* the bat, *landing* on the floor after jumping off the box, and *catching* the speeding heavy ball are the hardest, most fatiguing parts of these actions. I had a fencer once come to me after the last bout of a long day and say, "My head cuts were hitting the floor!" His deceleration muscles, the muscles that had to stop the blade, had become exhausted before his acceleration muscles, the muscles that "swing" the blade. Similarly, the muscles that stop your lunge may tire before the muscles that drive it. This is common because deceleration is a more difficult task.

    An athlete who adds heavy jumping, catching or swinging to a workout should be careful about the deceleration part of the exercise. Just being able to jump over an object, throw a ball, or swing a bat doesn't mean it's not too heavy a task. Landing, catching the ball, or stopping it with good form are also important.

A fencer needs rapid deceleration as well as acceleration.

Neural Novelty

    Specific, seemingly minute physical variables change how the body responds to exercise. For example, if the athlete changes the size or shape of the handle by which he or she grasps the weight, the body seems to think of the exercise as a whole new exercise. So athletes can challenge their nervous system simply by wrapping towels around the handles of the dumbbells, thereby making them fatter.

    Neural novelty is especially valuable for the experienced weightlifter whose body has become so comfortable with the exercises that it is refusing to make strength gains. Neural novelty can wake it up again. Neural novelty is also good for the athlete's mind: it can add an unexpected change of pace to a common workout.

    Another neural novelty wake-up call comes from putting the athlete in an unstable situation. Let's use the bench press again as an example. Suppose that you have been doing a 60-pound dumbbell bench press (30 pounds in each hand). At your next workout, your coach suggests 20 pound dumbbell bench presses (10 pounds in each hand) *on the Swiss ball.* The Swiss ball is an unstable surface that puts the athlete in genuine danger of rolling off the ball and falling onto the floor. This danger is what excites the athlete's body, which must summon more drive and more muscle in order to avert the impending fall while still accomplishing the lift. *It is the job of athletes and their coaches to design the instability danger so that it will not overwhelm the athlete and result in an actual fall!* This is the reason for *drastically decreasing the weight lifted* when first trying the unstable exercise. If the first set seems to be under control, the athlete can advance to larger weights in subsequent sets.

Improve your training by "fooling" your nervous system.

Design the instability danger so that it doesn't overwhelm you!

Section 2: The Program

As we have seen, all strength is not the same. Each different type of strength is like a different skill. And each sport has a fairly unique set of strength skills. Strength is properly developed by introducing the forms of overload to the athlete's body in a reasonable progression. We call this progression the four-phase program. Each phase of the training program stresses one set of exercise variables or forms of overload, as described in preceding chapters.

Phase 1: *Separate*—the Basic Conditioning Phase

Strength comes first from the basic forms of conditioning, many of them in the weight room, that are common to all sports. This is Phase 1 of this program. During Phase 1 the athlete works with variables such as time under tension, or weight, reps and sets. A beginning athlete has a lot of new skills to learn, so complexity and novelty are unavoidable issues. In Phase 1, the athlete is building body's "hardware," adding strength to muscles and connective tissue, adding blood vessels, and producing local muscle endurance. At the same time, the athlete is building the body's "software" by increasing and coordinating a muscle's response to nervous system signals.

Phase 2: *Integrate*—Add Balance and Coordination Skills

Once athletes reach a level of basic strength appropriate to their sport and age level they can begin to work the balance and whole-body coordination skills that are useful in their sport. This is Phase 2 of this program. In this phase, strength advancements come from the addition of neural novelty, skill complexity and instability to their exercise routine. The athlete's body adapts to this routine by increasing its skill to efficiently express strength under less ideal circumstances. Also the athlete's strength and local muscular endurance continue to develop.

Phase 3: *Accelerate*—Incorporate Speed and Agility

When an athlete has reached a level of balance and coordination appropriate to their sport and age level, he or she can begin to work on strength expressed through speed and agility. This is Phase 3 of this program. In this phase, strength advancements come from the addition of speed and deceleration challenges to the exercise routine. The athlete's body adapts to this routine by expressing its strength under conditions with more speed, change of direction and impact. Meanwhile, strength and local muscular endurance continue to develop, while connective tissue learns to deal with a new level of force from the high impact exercises.

Phase 4: *Incorporate*—Use Your Strength, Balance, and Speed in Sport-Specific Actions

Once an appropriate level of speed-strength and agility-strength is attained, an athlete should move on to the task of expressing strength through the skills and actions of his or her sport. This is Phase 4 of this program. In Phase 4, athletes must spend a lot of time and energy perfecting sport-specific skills. Thus they have less time and energy for strength training, so they now move into a strength maintenance program. In Phase 4, sport skill complexity and intense mental and emotional pressures drive the athlete's body and mind, and high speeds and impacts at competition intensity come into play as the skills are repeated over and over again. Under these circumstances, strength, speed and local muscular endurance are perfected and molded to the precise needs of their sport's movements.

These four phases of training cycle through every year of an athlete's training. An athlete is never done with any phase. You return each year to the weight room, to balance challenges, and to speed training in order to revive, adjust, build and perfect your strength.

The 4-phase program is a designed progression of overload. At each phase, the athlete's body responds to the overload by growing stronger in different ways. The phases of the program proceed in a logical order, stimulating the body first to build a foundation of strength, then to improve reactive stability, and finally to train the body to act powerfully, explosively, quickly and with agile change of direction.

There can be some overlapping between phases. For example, you can be working on the end of Phase 1 and beginning of Phase 2 at the same time. But never forget that the most satisfyingly strong feelings come when you progress step by step and enjoy the mastery of each exercise.

The Exercises and the Photos

Every exercise discussed in each section of the text that follows is demonstrated and summarized in the photos immediately following that section. The text will give an overall picture of each phase and all of its parts, offer an anatomy lesson when necessary, suggest combinations and connections between the exercises. The photos will give precise exercise directions and pointers and precautions about the exercise.

Phase 1: Separate!

Phase 1 is called *Separate* because it takes complex movements found in sports activities and separates them into simpler movements. In Phase 1 the athlete practices separate movements which are simpler than sports movements but not easy. This phase reduces complexity so the athlete can focus the body's resources on building a strong framework for later quick and complex moves. It is important that complexity is reduced, rather than eliminated. We are trying to create a smart body, so we present the body the challenge of exercises that are simple but not stupid.

Are you new to weightlifting? Are terms like clean, squat, bench press, row and (bodybuilder's) lunge unfamiliar to you? Is your only lifting experience on machines? If you answer "yes" to any of these questions, you should seek the advice of a qualified fitness trainer. Tell the trainer you want a solid foundation in how to do a clean, an overhead press, a squat, a bench press, a row and a lunge with free weights. If he or she doesn't know how to instruct you in free weights and tries to convince you to use machines, find another trainer. The following chapters will contain basic information on the purpose of these exercises and on how to avoid common errors.

Why free weights? Read on…

The Benefits of Free Weights

Free weights are better at producing functional strength than machines because they challenge your balance and the stability of your joints. If you use a machine, you are pushing a weight in a track. There is no possibility of it going any way but up or down. Hence, the muscles that would keep a real-life load from going left or right, forward or back, or round about can go to sleep during the lift. But these muscles must be prepared to act when the athlete enters the athletic arena! And this preparation can only be done with free weights.

Machines are in some sense foolproof. But if used properly, free weights are safe and they are much more effective. The keys to safe use of free weights are: don't lift more than you can handle *with good form*, don't lift to exhaustion (just to loss of good form), and always work with a spotter, someone who can help you with the weight if you can't control it or if you become too weak to continue.

> **Always work with a partner. Partner training is the only safe way to deal with free weights. Your partner should be available to help you— not in another room down the hall. Accidents happen even in the safest of circumstances, so always have available someone who can call for help. If you are doing something new your partner should stand nearby to spot your exercise. If you are doing very heavy barbell lifts, use two partners, one to spot each end of the bar. If you cannot get a partner, then you can use machines that will not allow the weight to fall on you. But remember: a spotter or a partner does not take the place of safe lifting practices as described throughout this book.**

Free weights give us a lot of variety in our training:

- by changing the way we use our legs, for example, lunge versus squat,
- by changing our body position, for example, over head press versus bench press,
- by changing from pulling to pushing, for example overhead press versus upright row,
- by changing the type of weight, for example, from barbell to dumbbell.

Cable Machines and Tubing

To go beyond the changes that free weights offer, we can use cable machines or rubber bands/tubing. Cable machines offer a great variety of pulling and pushing angles to the standing athlete. Cable machines are very expensive. An effective, less expensive substitute is offered by rubber tubes of different thicknesses that mimic a range of weight resistances and have a comfortable handle securely attached to each end. These can be secured to door frames or other weight apparatus such as a squat rack and used to imitate a cable machine. The two primary cable- or tube-based exercises in Phase 1 are the latissimus dorsi (lat) pulldown and the seated row. In Phase 2, as we'll see, they are even more important in the form of cable or rubber tube pulls and pushes. (Sources for purchasing the cables and other training equipment are listed in the Appendix.)

1.1 Basic Posture Exercises

The exercises in this section align and stabilize the joints, particularly the spine. These are not very exciting exercises, they don't contribute to beauty and you can't impress anyone by demonstrating them. All of my fencers are convinced these exercises wreck their stud factor and insist on doing them behind closed doors. *But they do contribute to sports excellence!* And they are essential to a long and healthy life. If you avoid them, your chance of having joint pain in the future is greatly increased.

The key to good exercise form is to have all your body parts stacked, one straight over the other. For standing posture, think of ears over shoulders over hips over ankles. Between the ears and the hips there are three curves: the cervical curve behind the neck, the thoracic curve behind the rib cage, and the lumbar curve behind the belly. The most acute problems arise in the lumbar region, but the thoracic curves and the neck suffer chronically from everything that goes wrong beneath them.

Stand with your back against the wall. Roughly speaking, your lumbar curve should be large enough for you to slip your flattened hand between the wall and your lower back. When you do any exercise, from something as simple as a push up, to something as complex as a squat, to something as dynamic as a power clean, you should *maintain that lumbar curve*. Don't hyperextend it by arching your back, and don't let it flex forward. For people with bad discs, flexion (forward bending) is particularly bad because it squeezes the discs backward toward the nerves.

The thoracic curve should be such that the shoulders and the ears all align vertically over the hips. Too many Americans have too much thoracic curve, either because they've done too many crunches or because they've spent too much time hunched over a table, a school desk, an auto steering wheel or a computer keyboard. Excess thoracic curve causes forward head lean, which in turn causes neck aches, headaches, and other problems.

The Cobra / Aquaman and the Pushup Extension

One way to help correct a chronic and excessive forward bend of the thoracic spine is the exercise called in some places the Cobra and in others the Aquaman. This exercise can be coupled with the thoracic spine extension stretch on the Swiss ball. It can also be combined with the single arm standing rubber band push and pull of Phase 2 to further mobilize the thoracic spine.

The Aquaman exercise teaches the athlete how to pull the shoulder blades in toward the spine, thus strengthening the rhomboid and lower trapezius muscles that anchor the shoulder blade during any *pulling motion*. The Pushup Extension strengthens the serratus muscles, which anchor the shoulder blades during any *pushing motion*. Together, the Aquaman and the Pushup Extension stabilize the shoulder and help to prevent wear and tear injuries to the shoulder joint.

The Four-Point Exercises

The athlete takes the Four-point stance (hands and knees) to do the Superman, Dynamic Superman and the Tummy Vacuum, or transverse abdominal activation exercise.

The Superman

Some athletes have had experience performing the Superman lying prone on the floor and lifting all four limbs at once. The advantage of doing the Superman in the four-point stance using only two limbs at a time is that you work the muscles and the spine the way that they commonly work. The forces run diagonally across the back and thereby teach the gluteus and hamstrings of the extended leg to work with the latissimus dorsi (lat) above the diagonally opposite (contralateral) leg. This is a common and functional combination called the posterior oblique system (see pp. 85–86 for further explanation). This exercise also works the small muscles of the back that are connected on both ends to the spine, such as the multifidus. These muscles learn to stabilize the spine against the alternating diagonal forces that the exercise produces.

The Dynamic Superman

The four-point Superman can be progressed by writing the alphabet in the air with the toe of the elevated foot. This sends mild shakes through the back, giving the muscles a more dynamic stabilization task. The exercise can be progressed still further by adding ankle and wrist weights to the elevated limbs. Finally the exercise can be progressed to the four-point Dynamic Superman where the athlete touches the knee and elbow of the extended limbs together under the body, then extends them out to the regular Superman position.

The Tummy Vacuum

The four-point stance Tummy Vacuum trains the transverse abdominal muscles. These muscles run around the belly and can be trained to pull in around the belly like a weight belt. When they are pulled in they support the vertebra and discs of the low back by tightening the thoraco-lumbar fascia, a sheet of very tough material across the lower back. But it's not enough to train the abdominal muscles! *Get into the habit of tightening them gently when doing all standing exercises.*

A Basic Balance Exercise: the Single Leg Stand

Balance exercises are also essential at the beginning of the athlete's training program. The single most indispensable balance exercise is the single leg stand (p. 49). It is included here in the posture section because the legs are the foundation of the pelvis, and the pelvis is the foundation of the spine. The legs are at the bottom of the structure, so when they shake, they very often send tremors up the structure, which the pelvis and the spine must learn to live with safely and effectively.

Single leg stands reduced ACL injuries in female soccer players by more than 85%.

The single leg stand is a great protector of the athlete's legs. A study of 900 female soccer players (300 in the control group) showed that the single leg balance exercise on the foam pad and on the floor with eyes closed reduced the incidence of injuries to the ACL (anterior cruciate ligament of the knee) by more than 85%. It also helps to protect the lower back by strengthening the muscles that keep the hips level during the exercise.

Illustrations

Phase 1.1: Basic Posture Exercises

Cobra / Aquaman

Thoracic Extension on Swiss Ball

Wall Reach-up

4-Point Stance Superman

4-Point Stance Dynamic Superman

4-Point Stance Tummy Vacuum

Pushup Extension

Single-Leg Stand

Cobra / Aquaman

Begin with the shoulders relaxed and touching the floor. Raise the ribs, squeeze the shoulder blades together, externally rotate the arms, and keep the head in line with the thoracic spine. Hold and then release. Since this is an isometric stabilizer exercise it is not done in reps but rather by holding for a time period. When you can hold the cobra for 2 minutes without shaking or losing position you are in good shape. Often one shoulder blade will begin to fall first.

Some athletes will raise the ribs by hyperextending the lumbar spine. This is incorrect. You should learn to raise the ribs by straightening the thoracic spine while keeping the lumbar spine relaxed. Remember to keep the chin down.

This is a basic posture exercise to strengthen the muscles that connect the shoulder blade to the spine as well as the muscles that connect the upper arm to the shoulder blade. You don't have to continually hold your shoulder blades together like a soldier at stiff attention. Normal posture is to have the shoulder blades relaxed. But you should have some tone in the muscles that pull the arms and blades back to help keep your shoulders in a healthy motion pattern during pulling actions in training and in sports.

Make progress in this area by moving on to the pulling exercises: the Bent-Over Row (p. 65), the Single-Arm Standing Cable Pull, (p. 90), and the Single-Arm, Single-Leg Band Pull, (p. 103.)

Thoracic Extension on Swiss Ball

Begin relaxed, with shoulder blades on the ball as shown. Let the arms externally rotate overhead. Let the front of the ribs rise up towards the chin. Roll back on the ball and activate the abdominal muscles. Let gravity extend the thoracic spine. Relax a few seconds and roll forward. Repeat five times.

Do not force this exercise. Be gentle. If there is pain, stop the exercise until the source of the pain is known. For some people with stiff backs, the ball may be too much curve. This is most likely with athletes over forty. If you find the ball to be too much curve, try simply lying back on the floor with feet flat on the floor (knees bent) and letting the arms externally rotate overhead and the ribs raise. After letting the arms rotate overhead for a few seconds times five repetitions, put your arms at your sides and relax for five or ten minutes, letting the back and shoulders relax into the ground.

Start by rolling back until the shoulder blades are across the top of the ball. Progress the exercise by hanging further over the back of the ball as shown. The wall reach-up is a companion exercise for improving posture in the thoracic spine. The wall reach-up is a progression of this exercise in that it integrates pelvic and lumbar spine posture with thoracic posture and shoulder flexibility.

Wall Reach-up

Begin by standing with your back to the wall. Tuck the chin in and place your butt, upper back and back of head against the wall. Bend your arms and raise them so the elbows point forward. Now straighten the arms overhead and get them as close to the wall as possible. Pull the belly in and up so the low back is as flat as possible. Hold for three seconds and relax. This is one repetition.

This is a stretching and a neurological exercise. Athletes with an inadequate range of motion in the shoulder and upper back need to teach their back and shoulders a new range of motion without over-extending the lower back. At the same time, they must learn to integrate proper thoracic extension with good lumbar posture. Often an athlete will hyperextend the lumbar spine to make up for lack of extension in the thoracic spine.

For some people, it will be a challenge to achieve a position with the elbows pronated forward without hyperextending the lumbar spine.

Repeat this exercise 5 times several times each day. To reprogram the body, it is better to get small exposures throughout the day rather than a long exposure (many reps and sets) once during the day. This exercise can be done almost anywhere, not just in the training room.

This exercise is not meant to be progressed.

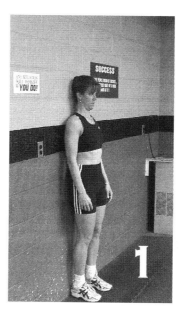

4-Point Stance Superman

Begin in the 4-point stance: hands under shoulders and knees under hips. Test your posture by placing a large dowel stick, curtain rod, etc. on your back. The stick should touch three points: at the sacrum, between the shoulder blades and on the back of the head. The first few times, it helps to have a partner spot for you. There should be enough space between the stick and the lumbar curve to allow the fingers to pass through. But if the whole hand can pass under the stick, the lumbar curve is too large. Touch your head to the stick by pulling your chin in rather than by rotating your cranium backwards.

Then raise one arm at a 45-degree angle to the stick and extend one leg parallel to the stick. Keep the shoulders and hips level, rather than, for example, raising the hip on the side of the extended leg.

This exercise trains the small muscles of the back (multifidus, etc.) and the oblique musculature to keep the spine in a neutral position while under stress. When these smaller muscles get tired, your form in this exercise will become erratic. It may be frustrating for an athlete who can run for miles to tire after 2 minutes of this exercise. Be patient. Work on it regularly. It will help both performance and health.

Progress this exercise by writing the alphabet with the heel of the raised leg. The letters should be a foot tall. It can also be progressed by adding small ankle and wrist weights.

Once you have learned the correct form, you can do this exercise without the stick.

4-Point Stance Dynamic Superman

Begin in the 4-point stance as described in the Superman exercise. Raise opposing arm and leg into the superman position. Bring the elbow and knee together beneath the body and return to a stable superman position. Do a certain number of repetitions with one arm and leg and then repeat the same number of repetitions with the other pair of limbs.

This exercise is done without the stick because you have to flex your spine at least a little, which would cause the stick to roll off. The key to this exercise is that the you return to a stable superman position with correct spinal curvature and horizontal hips and shoulders. You should become very proficient in the basic 4-point stance superman, holding the large dowel, before graduating to the dynamic superman exercise.

This exercise does develop some strength endurance but it is most importantly a neurological exercise. Therefore good form, by returning to a stable superman position after each repetition, is essential. With this goal in mind, the athlete should not exercise for longer than 60 seconds per set. This exercise can be progressed by adding small ankle and wrist weights.

4-Point Tummy Vacuum

Use a spotter when learning this exercise to ensure correct form. Begin by assuming the correct 4-point stance as described in the superman exercise. Inhale and push the belly out as far down to the floor as possible. Slowly exhale and draw the belly in. You should feel the tension of the transverse abdominus around to the low back. Now hold the lower belly in and breathe so that the upper belly moves out and in but the lower belly stays still. Relax and begin again. All this should be done with good spinal curves and contact points with the dowel as described in the superman exercise.

This seemingly odd little exercise is very important because many people have little or no control of their transverse abdominus. It takes many days of training before some athletes can communicate with their TA. Sometimes the athlete will mistakenly activate the rectus abdominus which runs from the ribs down to the pelvis. This is incorrect activation. Your spotter can see that you are using your RA by the fact that the belly is flat rather than slightly posterior to the ribs (concave) in the area of the belly button.

You can progress this exercise by doing it in a half squat with hands resting firmly on knees like a baseball short stop in the rest position between pitches. You can further progress it by doing it in the standing position.

Pushup Extension

Begin in the pushup position. Note that the shoulder blades are together towards the spine, indicated by the shadow of the inner margin of the shoulder blade visible in the photo. Next, push the shoulder toward the floor, so that the shoulder blades move away from the spine, and hold for 3 seconds. Then return to the beginning position. This is one repetition. 3 sets of 12 reps would be a good goal for this exercise.

Keep a neutral spine through out the exercise.

The motion exercises the serratus anterior, which stabilizes the shoulder girdle against pushes from the front (such as the floor pushing up into the shoulder through the arm when in the pushup position.) When in the pushup position, some athletes look like they have little bat wings sticking out of their back which is their shoulder blades being pushed out of position and their body hanging off of the blades. The pushup extension and the cobra exercise would be a complete shoulder girdle stability set for basic stability against pushes and pulls.

There is no need to progress this exercise. Once the SA muscles have been taught to hold the weight of the body, they will be able to participate correctly in other exercises such as the one arm cable push and will progress along with the other muscles of the athlete's body.

One-Leg Stand

> **This exercise is extraordinarily important for injury prevention. It should be thought of as a prerequisite for participation in a sport.**

This exercise is technically simple. Begin by standing on one leg. Then stay there for anywhere from 20-60 seconds. You should fight to stay up. Wobbling means that your body is learning how to deal with the uncertainty of the single leg base. But excessive wobbling means you have not yet mastered that particular level of the stand. You should be fairly still during the stand.

This exercise challenges the muscles that adjust the angle of the ankle, knee and hip. It also challenges the somatosensory system, that is, the parts of the body that can sense the position of the limbs. It is a strength exercise and a neurological exercise.

This exercise is progressed from standing on the floor with eyes open, to floor with eyes closed, to standing on the pad with eyes opened (pictured), to a pad while moving hands from side to side, to a pad with eyes closed. Once the athlete is solid in the progressions of the one leg stand and has gone through the basic leg strengthening exercises, they can progress their stability to a dynamic situation by attempting the lateral bound to one-leg stand.

1.2 Basic Weightlifting Exercises for Fencers

What are the basic movements of a competitor during the game or match? Rather than focusing on which muscles they want to get bigger in order to look better, like the bodybuilders, the sports athlete looks for increased strength and power in the movements they need. The following sections detail the lifts I believe to be essential to fencing and some basic advice on how to perform them.

Many people in our society work in a seated position for hours during the day. You may be one of them! Or you may have exercised predominantly with weight machines that guide you through a lifting motion. As a result, your movement skills may be underdeveloped.

> *If you are one of these people, or if you coach one, you must pay very close attention to form during the learning portion of the training program. A movement may seem simple, but that does not mean that an inexperienced athlete can do it without help from a proficient coach or trainer. Sometimes it takes several training sessions before you start to get it right.*

I have found that some athletes benefit from seeing themselves do the exercise on video. Then the coach can point out a deficiency such as, "See how your low back is rounding out?" Often the athlete can see what was wrong without the coach helping at all. Videotaping yourself (or sweet-talking someone else into doing it) is even more important if you don't have a coach. It can give you a view from outside yourself, which is essential to seeing deficiencies.

The Squat

The squat is the most essential lift.

The squat (pp. 60–61) is the most essential of the essential lifts. It teaches the athlete to combine posture and power. Some people call the posture of the squat "the ready posture" because the head and chest are up and the eyes are forward. In the squat, the feet are under the body; the legs bend to lower the body while the torso remains fairly erect. For fencers this is a good general description of the on guard position. When done correctly, the squat helps to build strength in the legs and the back and contributes to safety, efficiency and power in all similar motions) performed in the athletic arena—and there are many. We can't name all the muscles that are strengthened by the squat because it benefits almost all of them (except the arms). It is a total torso and leg strengthener.

The spine should stay neutral through the whole lift, not flexing or extending out of the normal thoracic and lumbar curves. There will be some forward lean from the hips as the athlete goes down but it should not bring the head forward beyond the feet. Hence the squat teaches neutral spine and upright ready posture, looking at the "opponent" and ready to go. At the same time, it teaches a limited forward lean in combination with an expression of power (controlling a heavy weight).

The squat posture is the foundation of all standing athletic movements. It is not easy to maintain good posture while squatting under even a small load. Even a lightweight squat will point out the athlete's weaknesses very quickly.

The key to a safe and effective squat, as with all other exercises, is to be strict with the athlete's form. Both the posture and the alignment of all the joints must be perfect.

> **Do not give in to the desire to move up in weight if your form is imperfect.** *There is always a tendency to advance the weight too soon. Resist it!*

Be sure the form is automatic and that the connective tissue has had time to catch up with muscle strength.

If you can, I highly recommend buying and using a safety squat bar in concert with a secure squat rack. This uniquely designed bar sits over the shoulders and stays there without you holding it. The same bar can also be used in the lunge. With this bar, the athlete's hands are free to be extended for balance. This way a safer, more upright position is possible. And if the athlete loses balance, the free hands can grab the squat rack to regain control.

If you don't have access to a safety squat bar, you can choose between two positions of the straight bar. In the more common position, the bar rests on the shoulders behind the neck; in the other, the bar rests on the shoulders in front of the neck with the elbows pointing forward to create a "shelf" for the bar. This is called the front squat. It allows for a more upright position of the spine during the lift. For some people, the front squat is the only way to keep good form during the exercise. In either case, I strongly recommend the use of a molded plastic device for distributing the weight of the bar over the back of the neck (for the behind-the-neck position) or over the shoulders (for the front position). These are readily available under the brand names Manta Ray and Sting Ray respectively. If the athlete is on a tight budget, towels over the front of the shoulders or across the upper back can be used to soften the pressure of the bar.

Buy a safety squat bar and a secure squat rack!

The Bench Press

The bench press is the beginning of your training in the pushing motion. When done correctly, the bench press helps to build strength in the whole shoulder complex and contributes to safety, efficiency and power in all pushing type motions done in the athletic arena. For fencers, the arm motions used in competition are such complex combinations of pushing, pulling and shoulder rotation that it makes no sense to separate out which motions are predominantly pushing motions. But there are obstacles to effective development of the shoulders with the bench press.

It is a common mistake to assume that you should bring the bar down to your chest no matter how much stress it puts on your shoulder joint. If you were standing, the push would be preceded by a backward (posterior) movement of the elbows, and your shoulder blades would move together towards the spine. But when you lie on the bench, the bench blocks the shoulder blades and keeps them square. You don't have sufficient range of motion in the shoulder joint itself to make up for the immobile shoulder blades. People assume that the shoulder joint with an immobilized shoulder blade can handle that range of motion. But that assumption may well be incorrect.

The main reason for this error is the "stud factor." The bench press is one of the most common contributors to an athlete's stud factor in the gym. And most studs consider it cheating not to lower the weight all the way to the chest. Thus they increase their reputation as studs at the expense of their shoulder joint. If lowering the bar all the way to the chest takes you past the terminal range of motion in your shoulder joint, you will be stretching out your shoulder capsule and decreasing its passive strength.

Don't bring the bar all the way down to your chest.

> **Test your shoulder joint while lying on the bench in order to learn the point at which the front of the shoulder joint becomes tight. This point should be the bottom of your bench press. Don't lower the weight any further!**

As a general rule, the coach can have each athlete stop when the upper arms go just below parallel to the floor. Later, when more developed, the athlete can do dumbbell bench presses on a Swiss ball, which will allow the shoulder blades to move back, allowing the athlete to bring the weight a little lower for a fuller range of motion.

One important caution with regard to the dumbbell bench press has to do with how you load them up:

If the weights are on the floor before the lift (as is all too common), the athlete will often sit on the bench and bend over to grab the weights off the floor. The result of flexing the spine this way is to put pressure on the lumbar discs— as much as 235% of the weight being lifted.

Instead, the athlete, especially those with lower back problems, should place the weights on boxes at the end of the bench before the exercise begins. The athlete should stand between the boxes and squat down to get the weights, then stand up and sit on the bench with the weights on their thighs, maintaining a good lumbar curve at all times.

When finished lifting, simply drop the weights onto the padded floor and then retrieve them when you stand up. (Notice that the padded floor is in this case a safety feature.) As with all exercises, don't increase the weight until the connective tissue has had enough time to catch up with the muscle strength.

Dead Lift

The dead lift is a great exercise for the legs and the back extensors. It contributes to safety, efficiency and power in other standing lifts such as the clean. In the sport of power lifting, super-strong weightlifters can accomplish their heaviest single lifts in the dead lift. For any athlete lifting to facilitate performance in another sport, the dead lift is an important exercise.

The dead lift is often used in combination with the upright row as a preparation for the clean. Here the athlete performs a dead lift, bringing the weight from the floor to a standing position with the arms hanging straight down. From this point the athlete immediately pulls up, completes an upright row, and then puts the weight back on the ground. Since the upright row is a weaker motion than the dead lift, which, as we said, is one of the strongest motions, this exercise is done with a very light weight relative to the dead lift and a normal weight relative to the upright row.

Bent-Over Row

Rowing is pulling. It is the generic action of pulling inward (toward the chest) with the arms, whether the pull is done while standing, sitting or bending over. The row is the beginning of the athlete's training in the pulling motion. When done correctly, rows help to build strength in the whole shoulder complex and contribute to safety, efficiency and power in all pulling motions. For fencers, the arm motions used in competition are complex combinations of pushing, pulling and shoulder rotation. The most important effect of the row for fencers is to build strength in the whole shoulder complex which reaches back all the way to the thoracic spine. The bent-over row is the athlete's introduction to all these movements.

Like all shoulder exercises, the bent-over row has two major movement components: (1) the movement of the upper arm around the shoulder joint; (2) the movement of the shoulder blade backward and inward toward the spine. These two parts should start and finish together. Begin this exercise with slow repetitions to be sure the shoulder blade gets a good firm squeeze towards the spine.

Avoid a violent, "yanking" motion that throws the shoulder blades toward the spine. This yanking form tends to produce a relative weakness in the muscles that pull the shoulder blades together, leaving them too weak to control posture and keep the shoulder blades from slumping forward. If it is impossible to correctly control the shoulder blade, the athlete should go back to the Aquaman and the four-point Superman described in the section on posture.

Another common type of bad rowing form is the bent back. Many people bend the back far forward when bending over to do the bent-over row. This is simply wrong. Don't let the lower back lose its lumbar curve! And don't let the normal curve of the thoracic spine go forward and make the head jut forward. This is all easier said than done. It is easy to see bad posture but it is difficult to feel it, especially when doing a new motion or a new exercise. So when doing this exercise, you need a spotter, or at the very least a mirror. Then, when you are asking yourself, "Is it a neutral spine yet?" your spotter, or your mirror, can tell you, "No—it's still hunched over."

In the single-arm row, which is a progression of the bent-over row, the unweighted arm reaches forward while the weighted arm pulls back. When done correctly, the single-arm row helps to increase the mobility of the thoracic spine. This is particularly helpful for older athletes because the thoracic spine naturally loses flexibility with age. The athlete tries to make up for loss of thoracic spine mobility with increased shoulder mobility. But exaggerated shoulder mobility can result in strains and sprains and other maladies of the shoulder.

Be sure to perform bent-over rows with good posture, and avoid doing them with an overly heavy weight. It is a great temptation to go heavy, but it tends to mess up your posture, pulling you excessively forward. And it tends to throw off the coordination of the shoulder blade moving toward the spine with the upper arm moving toward the shoulder blade.

Upright Row and Lat Pulldown

The upright row and lat pulldown are, like the bent-over row, pulling exercises. The shoulder has such a great variety of motions that it can pull in three different directions. The point of exercising in all three directions in a strength training program is not that all three are used in any one sports movement but rather that the exercises solidify the shoulder in three directions. Balanced strength in all directions makes the shoulder generally healthier and more resistant to injury.

> *One important caution for each of these exercises:*
> *Contrary to the suggestion of some bodybuilders, the upright row should end when the elbow reaches shoulder level, <u>not when the bar reaches shoulder level.</u> This keeps the shoulder from binding at the top of the motion, an action called impingement. And, no matter what anyone says, <u>the lat pulldown should not be pulled down behind the neck</u>. The bar should always be pulled down in front of the head, toward the upper chest. If the bar is pulled down behind the head the neck must crane forward and the shoulder joint must strain into extreme external rotation. Neither of these are good things to teach the body to do; nor are they healthy to even do a few times.*

Since we don't do any downward pulling in fencing, you might think that lat pulldowns are minimally important to fencers. But the lats (latissimus dorsi) and the other downward pulling muscles of the shoulders are important to the health of the shoulder and to the overall health of the body. The shoulder is a joint with huge mobility compared to other joints in the body. It gets this mobility by having a shallower and less restrictive socket. There is not much of a depression for your shoulder to stay put in when you move it around. The shoulder relies on the surrounding muscles to pull at the right time and keep the head of the upper arm bone from being bounced around in the shoulder joint. This increased mobility is a potential source of instability and injury. If our hips had as shallow a socket as our shoulders, they would have an amazing range of motion, but we would be weak and wobbly creatures! There are a lot of uses for a highly mobile shoulder, so we accept the compromise.

Shoulder stability—and injury avoidance—come from a balance between downward pulling strength and upward pulling strength. So you should try to keep your upward *and* your downward pulling shoulder muscles in shape.

The Clean

In the clean (p. 63), the athlete drives upward with the legs to lift the barbell from the ground, then, at the precisely correct moment, drops under the weight and stabilizes it at shoulder level. Learn the parts of the clean and get the form perfect.

In Phase 1, you must keep the weights light for the clean.

We call a heavy clean a "power clean" and include it in Phase 3. To be performed safely, the power clean requires considerable proficiency in the dead lift and the upright row, as well as basic ability in the clean. You need to give your shoulders and your back time to strengthen and mature before you try to make a heavy weight fly up to your shoulders as the power clean requires.

In addition, the clean is particularly tough on the upper back (trapezius) and the shoulders. Unlike the upright row or dead lift, where the weight hangs down from a stationary torso, the clean starts with leg drive while the athlete is bent over the barbell. The leg drive forces the pelvis and the torso up. But the weight has inertia. If it's a heavy weight, it has a lot of inertia. It doesn't want to go up. So the leg drive, which blasts upward while the weight is still hanging down, stretches the trapezius and stresses the shoulders as they begin to pull up.

When you're first learning the clean, you should practice just the form without any weight, in order to master the coordination. Then you can practice with an empty bar. Sometimes a certain part of the exercise presents a stubborn obstacle to good form. When the bar is light, beginners have a tendency to keep their elbows down and use their biceps when raising it toward their shoulders. This will not work as the weight gets heavier. Thus this part needs to be practiced by itself over and over again.

Later, the whole exercise can be performed with a lightly weighted bar.

The Simple Overhead Press

Pushing an object overhead is a common human endeavor and the shoulders are designed to accomplish this task But how do we justify the overhead press as a movement necessary for fencers? Pushing a weight up and then holding it there isn't much like a head parry in saber! The answer for fencers is that balancing the weight overhead evens out the strength in your shoulders and builds strength in the torso. This balance component is an essential feature of the overhead press's positive effect.

The Wall Reachup Exercise

Some athletes lack appropriate range of motion in the shoulders and upper back. Most commonly their upper back has so much forward lean that they cannot get their shoulder blade vertical. As a result, they can't get their shoulder joint vertical either. These athletes tend to hyperextend the low back in order to get the weight overhead. Therefore, they should frequently practice the *wall reachup exercise* as shown in the photos on p. 44.

> *If for any reason you can't straighten your thoracic spine no matter how many wall reach ups you might do,* avoid the overhead press. *It may damage your shoulder joint. You may be a fine athlete, but you should avoid the "wear and tear" problems that an incorrect position can cause.*

The simple overhead press executed in Phase 1 is connected to the dynamic overhead press of Phase 3. In the dynamic overhead press, you use your legs to get the weight started upward. The momentum enables you to get a heavier weight overhead. But it is your torso and arms that must stabilize the weight, and you build stability by practicing the simple overhead press of Phase 1.

The Lunge

The lunge is the beginning of the athlete's training in the lunging motion. Here one foot is in front and the other far behind. The front leg takes the majority of the body weight and the torso remains fairly erect. When done correctly, the lunge helps to build strength in the legs and back and contributes to safety, efficiency and power in all lunging type motions.

The lunge is, of course, a leg exercise. As such, it may seem redundant in a program that begins with the squat. In fact the lunge is much more taxing to the back of the leg and the butt than the squat. The lunge is necessary to build full strength and explosiveness in the rear of the leg. Also, it is a single leg exercise that taxes stability of the hip and knee joint, and the stability of the athlete's spine from side to side. The lunge is primarily a strengthening exercise but has a significant skill component. The first move in the lunge is the deceleration phase or lowering the weight where the action muscles are elongating while holding the weight. In any exercise this is the most strenuous phase if it is done with control.

It shouldn't be necessary to explain the importance of the lunge to fencers!

Some Additional Exercises:
Calf Strength, Shoulder Rotation and Shoulder Blade Support

In each sport, there may be a few places where the basic lifts do not reach all of the muscle groups necessary for producing all the sports movements. In the case of fencing, I believe the basic movements miss the calves, the shoulder rotators and the support muscles of the shoulder blade.

Calf Raises

The calf contains two major muscles and a bunch of minor but essential muscles that control the ankle. The major muscles are the soleus and the gastrocnemius, which is commonly called the "gastroc" for short. The gastroc crosses both the knee and the ankle while the soleus crosses only the ankle.

The ankle is a complicated joint which is the foundation of the whole body and does much of its work with the foot flat on the ground. But in the gym and on the practice floor the ankle is exercised mostly with the foot on the toes, as in the calf raise. So functionally, calf raises are less than ideal. But in Phase 1, where the goal is to strengthen connective tissue and blood supply and so on, calf raises are just fine. The athlete should use them to encourage the body to build a strong Achilles tendon.

Fencers should do double and single leg calf raises to strengthen the connective tissue of the ankle. Later they can advance to lateral hops to challenge the ankles at different angles and with greater velocity. It is best to do the calf raise with the foot hanging off a step of some sort. This way, the ankle can be lowered below the level of the toe. This works the ankle in its fully extended position.

A Word on PNF Shoulder Rotations

PNF is a system that strengthens and stabilizes the muscles, joints, and tendons.

I'm going to be a little technical here, because I want you to understand the source of a potentially devastating injury—and how to avoid it.

First of all, PNF stands for "proprioceptive neuromuscular facilitator." You can see why we use the abbreviation. The proprioceptors are sensitive receptors in the muscles, tendons, and joints that monitor body motion and position. PNF is defined as a system for facilitating the response of neuromuscular mechanisms by stimulating the proprioceptors. The PNF shoulder rotations strengthen and stabilize the muscles that rotate the shoulders.

The shoulder rotators are a group of small muscles that extend from the anterior and posterior sides of the shoulder blade to the upper end of the upper arm bone. They not only rotate the arm but also participate in some lifting motions. The rotator cuff—as in "So and so tore his rotator cuff"—is the place where the shoulder rotators connect; it provides stability and strength to the shoulder. Not only are the rotators small, they are very short compared to the arm that they are trying to rotate. The length of the smallest rotator is one inch and the length of the arm is 20. If you are trying to rotate a weight at the end of your arm—for example, when throwing a baseball or riposting from a head parry—you are using a one-inch lever to move a 20-inch arm. The force exerted by—and on— that one-inch rotator muscle is 20 times that of a weight—let's say a baseball—held in the hand at the end of a dangling arm

The result is that the rotator muscles and the rotator cuff are prone to stresses, pains and injuries. In the short run, they are a common source of very bothersome "referred pain" that shoots up to the neck and down into the arm. In the long run, after these extreme forces have been generated over many years, these muscles can get many small partial tears resulting in inflammation, pain and severe shoulder dysfunction. If at any time you experience shoulder pain, get help from a qualified muscle therapist. If the muscle therapist can't help they should be able to refer you to an orthopedist. Train wisely and get help early if you experience discomfort!

The rotators are critical to arm strength in fencing because the fencer must often express strength in the arm when it's rotated away from its most powerful positions. They are best exercised with what is called the PNF shoulder rotation movements. Begin with unweighted sets of the movements. (Unweighted movements can also be part of a team warm-up.) Then add small weights and slowly build strength. You can also pull rubber bands in parts of the range of motion where the weight is ineffective.

Rotator cuff muscles will never be equal in strength to the larger muscles in the body. Never force the shoulder to go beyond its natural range of motion by letting weights or rubber bands pull your arm. Keep a proper range of motion and teach your body to feel this range as your position of power.

> *In all cases let the whole body participate: let the shoulder blades move, let the torso and thoracic spine rotate. Do not overly isolate the rotators as they are small and need the help and cooperation of other body parts from the beginning of their training*
>
> *Never try to do a heavy weight or a 1RM with any shoulder rotation exercise. Rotator cuff muscles should always be exercised with very low percentages of 1RM. The exercises should be pain free. In the event of pain stop the exercise until you know the source of the pain.*

Shoulder rotation is one of the weakest motions that the body can do. We should teach our bodies to work around that weakness by utilizing PNF motions of the shoulder, and pushing and pulling with a cable as well.

Other Shoulder Stabilizers

The muscles that stabilize the shoulder *blades* and put them in the proper positions to facilitate the shoulder joint are often overlooked totally in strength training. These are the muscles that reverse the thoracic curve, the muscles that pull the shoulder blades towards the spine (rhomboid and lower trapezius) and the muscles that hold the fronts of the shoulder blades against the rib cage (serratus). For the first two the athlete should become proficient at the Aquaman/Cobra exercise (p. 42). For the latter, the athlete should be able to do the pushup extension (p. 48).

Illustrations

Phase 1.2: Basic Weightlifting Exercises for Fencers

Bench Press

Box-Assisted Squat

Front Squat

Dead Lift

Clean

Lunge

Bent-over Row

Lat Pulldown

Overhead Press

Step Up and Over

Calf Raise

Upright Row

PNF Shoulder Rotation #1

PNF Shoulder Rotation #2

Bench Press

Begin by taking the bar from the rack and raising it over your chest. Lower it, then lift it back up. This is one repetition.

For the average person, the lowest point on the lift should be when the elbows have come down to the level of the shoulders. Some people might suggest that the bar should come down to touch the chest. But bringing the bar down to the chest is injurious to the shoulder joint in the long run —it stretches out the front of the shoulder joint.

The bench press is predominantly a strengthening exercise, although at first it will be a skill challenge to beginners. It works the shoulders and arms and the muscles that reach from the shoulder across the chest to the sternum.

The bench press is a basic skill of weight lifting. When done correctly, it seems to have good overall effects on the whole body, stimulating it to greater strength gains. It is an exercise that young lifters should master and can feel good about. Further progressions of this exercise include: two dumbbells on a bench, a single dumbbell on a bench, two dumbbells with the back on a Swiss ball, a single dumbbell with the back on a Swiss ball. When starting a new form of the bench press, always decrease the weight. Before progressing to bench presses on a Swiss ball, the athlete should master some basic Swiss ball exercises, especially the supine hip extension (p.70).

Box-Assisted Squat

This exercise is performed with a support box placed a few feet behind the athlete, as shown in the photos.

Begin by standing up underneath the bar to lift it from the rack. Step backwards away from the rack using small steps. Be careful! Most accidents happen while stepping into or out of the rack. Line up with the box and stand in the ready position, feet spread, spine neutral, head erect, abdominals activated.

Squat down and touch the box. Rise up from the box to a standing position. Beginners may also place their full weight on the box to help them learn the proper way to get in and out of the lowest point with good form. Down and up is one repetition.

The squat is predominantly a strengthening exercise but it has a significant skill component because it is a challenge to maintain good posture during the lift. Many people think of this as a quadriceps exercise but many other body areas such as calves, front of shin, spinal erectors and abdominals have essential parts to play. The squat has whole body effects that increase the strengthening effects of other exercises. If the beginning to advanced athlete doesn't have much time to spend in a workout this exercise is one that produces much benefit in a short period of time.

These photos are shown using the Manta Ray, a form-fit plastic guard that attaches to the bar to protect the spine and shoulders from the bar.

Progress this exercise by increasing weight. Never go so heavy that you lose perfect form and control of the weight.

Front Squat

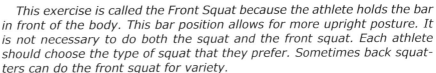

This exercise is called the Front Squat because the athlete holds the bar in front of the body. This bar position allows for more upright posture. It is not necessary to do both the squat and the front squat. Each athlete should choose the type of squat that they prefer. Sometimes back squatters can do the front squat for variety.

Begin by standing up underneath the bar to lift it from the rack. Step backwards away from the rack using small steps. Be careful! Most accidents happen while stepping into or out of the rack. Stand in the ready position, feet spread, spine neutral, head up, abdominals activated.

Squat down, then rise up to a standing position. Go down as far as you can while maintaining good form, but no lower than thighs parallel to the ground. Down and up is one repetition.

These photos are shown using the Sting Ray, a two-piece, form-fit plastic guard that attaches to the bar to protect the front of the shoulders from the bar and to make the bar sit securely on the shoulders.

This is predominantly a strengthening exercise but it has a significant skill component. Many people think of this as a quadriceps exercise but many other body areas such as calves, front of shin, spinal erectors and abdominals have essential parts to play. The squat has whole body effects that increase the strengthening effects of other exercises.

Dead Lift

The dead lift is a very simple exercise, but it takes a surprising amount of time to get the form perfect and consistent. Start with the barbell on the floor with your shins almost touching the bar. Grab the bar and stand up, letting the bar hang straight down from your shoulders. Then lower it back to the floor. You must do all this with a flat back and your head and chest up.

Avoid using a flexed back in this exercise. Keep the back straight or a little extended (bent backward). Also avoid locking out the knees before the back is vertical. The back and the legs should finish the lift at the same time.

Throughout the lift, your hips should be above your knees and below your shoulders. Since you start with the barbell on the floor the weight must be in front of your shins at the start. Thus you naturally lean forward more during the accomplishment of this exercise than, for example, the squat; therefore, you put more tension on your back extensors.

This exercise can also be done as a hanging dead lift. This means that after taking the weight off the floor the first time, in every subsequent repetition you lower the weight only to your knees (rather than all the way back to the floor) and then stand up again.

The dead lift strengthens the back, the butt, the legs and the shoulders. You can progress the dead lift to a combination lift. Start with a hanging dead lift and then, at the top of the dead lift, immediately execute an upright row. Then return to the bottom of the hanging dead lift. This is one repetition of a combination lift.

Clean

The exercise has four parts, which must be synchronized: (1) Flex the knees with the arms hanging down, (2) push the floor away, (3) pull the elbows straight up towards the ceiling and point the toes, (4) relax the ankles, flex the knees, drop the elbows and cradle the weight on the front of the shoulders. This combination of moves is done at a quick pace so one part of the lift feeds energy into the next. But you could practice it with pauses after each part to help to memorize the mechanics of the lift.

The primary energy of this lift is up. If you lean back prematurely you will be pulling the weight off its upward course towards the back. You should feel like you are doing a combination of jumping up and pulling up. Everything is up to the ceiling.

Don't be overanxious to go to heavy weights if you are new to the exercise. Do 20-repetition sets until you are very comfortable with the move and you are sure your shoulders are strong enough to progress to higher weights.

Progress the clean to a combination lift of the clean followed by the overhead press. This combination is different from the dead lift/upright row combination mentioned on the dead lift page in that it is normal to pause after the clean and summon your forces for the overhead press. The clean also progresses to the heavier version called the Power Clean, which is found in Phase 3.

Lunge

Begin by standing with the ball in front of your chin. Step forward and drop down. Stay upright and keep the hips level. Keep the front knee at roughly a 90 degree angle. Push backward and stand up, returning to the original position this is one repetition.

The athlete is shown holding a twenty pound medicine ball. Holding the ball this way also exercises all the muscles that internally rotate the shoulders. The lunge can also be done with body weight or with dumbbells.

Keep each knee pointed in the same direction as its attached foot. The calf should stay near perpendicular to the floor. Keep the upper body aimed up rather than lying forward on the front thigh. Train your head to stay up by doing the lunges while balancing a beanbag on your head.

Your hips may tend to tilt down on the side where the leg is back. This is a critical instability that affects both the knee and the lumbar spine. Try to go into and out of the lunge with a minimum of hip wobble or tilt.

The exercise is progressed by adding weight. It is also progressed in skill by lunging backward, by doing a walking lunge in which the athlete recovers forward, and by doing a lunge while moving the weight from side to side. These skill-oriented progressions make the exercise a neurological exercise. The only thing they demand of the body is more coordination to control the posture in and out of the lunge.

Bent-Over Row

Begin by flexing the knees and bending forward, keeping a good neutral spine, head in line with the spine and abdominals activated. Pull the weights straight up and lower them down. This is one repetition.

In a healthy pulling motion such as the row, the shoulder blades move towards the spine and the arms move posteriorly. Be sure that the athlete is accomplishing both. Sometimes the shoulder blades do not fully retract. This may be because of lack of skill, in which case you should practice the cobra exercise. Or it may be because the weight is too heavy, in which case you should work with a lighter weight. There should also be a good lumbar curve. Don't let the back flex over or hyperextend.

This exercise should not be done dynamically, that is, throwing heavy weights up with a little help from the back and legs. Instead, perform the lift carefully so that each muscle in the chain can learn to do its job.

This is primarily a strengthening exercise but has a significant skill component.

Progress this exercise by adding weight, but do not lift too much weight. Instead, progress the exercise neurologically by moving to such things as the one-arm bent-over row, and later, the one-arm cable pulls.

Lat Pull-Down

The lat pull is accomplished on a cable machine. It can also be accomplished using rubber tubing and an attachment to anchor the tube in a closed door. Adjust the seat and leg pads so that your arms are fully extended. Begin with the arms overhead. Pull the bar down in front of the head. This raises the weight at the other end of the cable. Extend the arms upward to full extension. This is one repetition.

Pulling the bar down behind the head is stressful to the neck and shoulders and should be absolutely avoided.

This is primarily a strengthening exercise. The lat pull uses some of the same muscles as the bent over row but helps to stabilize the shoulder in a different plane of motion. And, as the name implies, it exercises the latissimus dorsi, a muscle that runs from the upper arm to the low back. (This answers the question, "How is your arm connected to your low back?")

This exercise is progressed by adding weight. Chin-ups use the same muscles, but move the body towards the hands. Thus they are neurologically different exercises and can benefit the athlete by providing variety. A counterbalanced chin-up machine takes some weight off the athlete's arms and is an excellent machine for people who cannot as yet lift their own bodyweight.

Overhead Press

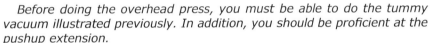

Before doing the overhead press, you must be able to do the tummy vacuum illustrated previously. In addition, you should be proficient at the pushup extension.

Begin in the split stance, toes pointed roughly forward with one foot a little ahead of the other. Begin with just a barbell (in the photo the athlete is using an empty Olympic bar, which weighs 45 pounds) at the shoulders. Push the weight overhead. Return to shoulder level. This is one repetition.

The weight in this exercise should not so heavy enough that you have to use your legs to bounce the weight from your shoulders.

While performing the overhead press, keep the transverse abdominus firm in order to stabilize the joints of the lower spine. If you do not, this exercise tends to produce hyperextension of the lower spine, and this can cause persistent problems.

This is a strengthening exercise with an essential balance component. Holding the weight overhead challenges the balance. The true strength expressed in this exercise is not just the ability to push a weight, but the ability to <u>control</u> it. The movement is actually rather common in real life: for example, putting a loaded box onto a high shelf in a closet.

The overhead press is progressed by adding weight. It can also be progressed to more unstable forms: two dumbbells pressed overhead together, two dumbbells alternately, or one dumbbell.

Step-Up and Over

Begin with the right foot on the box and the left foot on the floor. Step up onto the box but don't put the left foot down. Step off the far side of the box with the left foot, eventually standing on the left foot with the right toe still on the box. Reverse the process stepping backward onto the box and then backward onto the floor. This is one repetition. Repeat with each leg.

Maintain perfect posture throughout. Sometimes the precarious balance of the exercise will bring out the worst in the athlete's posture. (For example, in photo number 3, the athlete has moved his head forward a bit as he steps off of the box!) This exercise gives the athlete a dynamic situation in which to fortify good posture.

Overall the athlete spends a great amount of time on one leg. This is a balance and control exercise that takes a considerable amount of strength to accomplish. This exercise can be used as part of a strength routine or a balance routine.

This exercise can be progressed by doing the exercise while holding a medicine ball. Use heavier weights by holding a dumbbell in each hand. Once you progress to heavy weights, you should eliminate the step over part of the exercise. Simply step up onto the box and put the stepping foot down on the box to gain balance. Then step backwards returning to the floor. Repeat with both legs. An accelerated form of this exercise is the step-up jump.

Calf Raise

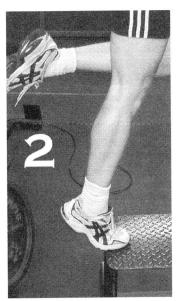

Begin by standing with your foot on a firm platform with the heel below the toe, hanging over the edge. Point the toe and flex the ankle, raising the whole body in the process. Lower the heel to the original position. This is one repetition.

You may keep a hand or a finger on a solid object in front of you to help their balance. Beginners or people who have been away from training for a while may begin with a two-leg raise, both toes on the platform, both calves exercising simultaneously. Either way it is a good idea to stretch the calf after performing the calf raise.

The calf raise strengthens the connective tissue of the ankle. The ankle needs to be <u>tough</u>, because it takes all the forces that come from above. And the ankle needs to be smart, because it is the first link in the chain of balance. All single leg exercises, such as the one leg stand and the step up and over, can be considered ankle intelligence exercises as well.

This exercise is progressed by performing the exercise while holding a medicine ball. Performing the exercise with a flexed knee while keeping the shin vertical is another important variation. To perform the flexed knee version the athlete should hold onto a firmly anchored object to help with balance. The ankle does not have any Phase 2 or Phase 3 exercises of its own because it simply blends into the overall function of the leg. But the dot drill (p. 130) s the accelerating exercise that most directly challenges the ankle.

Upright Row

Stand in a neutral posture, being sure not to let the weight pull the shoulders and head forward. Pull the weight up the centerline of the body until the elbows are level with the shoulders. Lower the weight. This is one repetition.

Some instruction manuals will suggest that the bar should be brought up to the collar bone. This is not ideal. Raising the elbows much past shoulder height causes the head of the arm bone to bang against the "ceiling" of the shoulder joint. Repeated practice of this banging may cause shoulder trouble. Also avoid the tendency to lean back and stick your head forward to lift a heavy weight. Reduce the weight if necessary. You must remain upright.

This is an upward pulling exercise for the shoulder area. As an upward exercise, it is grouped with the overhead press. As a pulling exercise, it is grouped with the lat pull and bent-over row. It exercises the upper trapezius (pulling the shoulder toward the ear) and the deltoids (pulling the elbow up and out.)

This is primarily a strengthening exercise. It helps to prepare the shoulder for accelerating activities that come later in the program. This exercise is progressed by adding reps and sets. Do not progress the weight too quickly or your form will degrade and the positive effect of the exercise will decrease.

PNF Shoulder Rotation #1

The photos here illustrate the beginning and the end position of PNF shoulder rotation #1. Begin in a position in which you look like you are about to draw a sword from its scabbard. Then move your arm out and rotate the shoulder externally until you are in the football passing position. Then return to the beginning position. This is one repetition.

This motion rotates the shoulder through a wide variety of shoulder positions from in toward the midline to out away from the midline. The normal range of rotation is to have the forearm straight up and down when in the football passing position and at a 45 degree angle down, when in the sword drawing position. But do not strain to gain these angles; do what is natural for you. And do not stretch past these angles; <u>more is not better</u>.

The shoulder rotators are small muscles with difficult leverage points on the bones. They do not take brutality nearly as well as the giants like the quadriceps.

This exercise should be smooth and pain free. If there is any sort of noise or pain, try to adjust the position of the exercise. If the pain or noise remains stop the exercise until the source of the rough or painful motion is known.

The exercise is shown freehand but can be progressed by adding weights in single pound increments. It is then progressed to the shoulder rotation with bands.

PNF Shoulder Rotation #2

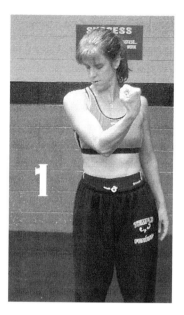

   The photos here illustrate the beginning and the end position of PNF shoulder rotation #2. Begin in the position where you look like you are showing off your biceps muscle. Then move your arm out and rotate the shoulder internally until your elbow is above your hand and you are pushing back with your open hand. Then return to the beginning position. This is one repetition.

   In this motion the hand is crossing diagonally from inside and up to out and down. When combined with shoulder rotation #1 the hand draws a large X.

   This motion exercises shoulder rotation in a wide variety of shoulder positions from in toward the midline to out away from the midline.

   The shoulder rotators should not be worked hard and heavy. They are small muscles with difficult leverage points on the bones. They do not take brutality nearly as well as the giants like the quadriceps.

   The exercise should be smooth and pain free. If there is any sort of noise or pain try to adjust the position of the exercise. If the pain or noise remains stop the exercise until the source of the rough or painful motion is known.

   The exercise is shown freehand but can be progressed by adding weights in single pound increments. It is then progressed to the shoulder rotation with bands.

1.3 Abdominal Development

The abdominal muscles are quite complex and allow human beings to do many wonderful and complicated things with their limbs. God made the abs with four muscle groups and eight major nerves servicing them, which is three more muscles than you need to do crunches, and eight more nerves than you need to sit in front of the TV and spasm under an electrostimulation belt! The abs are wired up to perform complex movements and functions for the service of sports performance and injury prevention. But the abs and the abdominal nervous system require training.

The Rectus Abdominus (RA)

The muscle that runs straight down the middle front of the belly is the rectus abdominus (RA). Everyone exercises these with crunches or sit-ups. They are the source of the famed "six-pack abs." They are the most over-exercised abdominal muscles—to the point where exercising produces negative effects in some athletes. An over-exercised RA tends to pull the rib cage down, aggravating the tendency in some people to have an excessive curve in the thoracic spine (upper back). An overly tense and active RA also tends to restrict healthy belly breathing. The athlete is left to breathe with the shoulders and some accessory breathing muscles in the neck. This tends to aggravate neck and shoulder pains.

All this trouble starts with too many crunches from the floor. To avoid this trouble:

- The RA should be exercised in proportion to the other four abdominal muscles
- It should be exercised in a variety of movements and
- *Athletes should do their crunches on the Swiss ball.* (This allows for full extension of the spine and teaches the abs to control the spine through its full range of motion.)

When people think of the abdominal muscles, they tend to think of the front of the body. They think of exercising the abs as exercising their belly. But in fact three of the four abdominal muscles reach around the side of the body and connect to the lower back. This means that *the abdominal muscles are lower back muscles as well.* The three abdominal muscles that connect to the lower back are described below.

The Transverse Abdominus (TA)

The least understood of all the ab muscles is the transverse abdominus (TA). The TA runs perpendicular to the spine in a sheet that attaches to the fascia on the lumbar (lower back) spine and runs forward to the center-line of the front of the body. Since it runs perpendicular to the spine, it pulls the belly straight in when it contracts. It is wired up so that different sections can contract separately: you can have the part of the TA below the belly button pulled in while the area above the belly button is relaxed and extended. What is the purpose of pulling the belly straight in, besides belly dancing? For one thing, it pulls the fascia on the lumbar spine taut, which provides low back support. In addition, it keeps the abdominal cavity under pressure during weight-bearing activities. Thus, intra-abdominal pressure becomes a *lifting* force, taking some compression force away from the lumbar spine. This is a natural action: think of holding your breath and squeezing your belly when trying to lift something heavy. Your body naturally employs the air and water pressure in the torso to help with the lift.

High blood pressure? See your doctor.

Don't "squeeze down" by sealing your lips.

> **One important caution: this natural compression raises the blood pressure! People with high blood pressure <u>must</u> ask their doctors whether their cardiovascular systems are in good enough shape to squeeze down during lifting. And even if your cardiovascular system is healthy, I recommend that you never squeeze down by** sealing **your lips as you squeeze your belly. Always release air through pursed lips. This allows a little pressure to support the spine but takes some pressure off of the cardiovascular system. Get in this habit of releasing pressure so you will do it automatically even if you're just lifting a bag of concrete in your yard. The least inter-abdominal pressure while still using some TA activation is produced by pulling in the lower half of the TA while not even pursing the lips but rather maintaining normal breathing.**

The Internal and External Obliques (IO and EO)

The internal and external obliques (IO and EO) are also sheet muscles that run diagonally around each side of the belly. They are involved in many basic functional abilities found in sports such as twisting and flexing to the side. They also stabilize the pelvis under the stresses of sports action and therefore stabilize the lower back. The IO runs at an angle roughly from the lower front ribs, down and around the same side from which it originates (these muscles do not cross the anterior midline of the body) to the bottom of the low back. The EO runs at an angle roughly from the front of the pelvis, up and around the same side from which it originates, to the lower ribs in the back of the body. In other words, the IO and EO crisscross on the sides of the body.

It's not well known, but the transverse abdominus and the external obliques can stabilize the pelvis while letting the rectus abdominus relax so as to allow belly breathing. (By the way, I am not saying that the athlete should never use the RA. However, *during times of low to medium stress in a sporting event, you can take more efficient belly breaths without sacrificing spinal stability.*) You can teach your abs this skill by practicing the lower abdominal exercises shown in the pictures on the following pages). After mastering these exercises, you can begin to concentrate on stabilizing your pelvis under weightlifting, plyometric and sports competition conditions.

Many exercises for the various ab muscles involve twisting and crunching. This is problematic in two ways. First, fencers, like many other athletes, do not perform a lot of actual twisting and crunching motions but rather use the trunk primarily to stabilize the limbs through a series of complex motions. Second, people with low back problems can damage their spinal discs by twisting, especially when combined with crunching.

Low back pain? See your doctor before doing twisting exercises.

> **In all cases, people with low back problems must get permission from a physician to do twisting exercises.**

The solution to both of these problems with twisting exercises is for the athlete to do abdominal exercises that *stabilize* the body against twisting and bending forces. These stability-oriented exercises teach the athlete with a bad back to protect the spine. They teach all fencers *to keep a stable torso—a base for good weapon control.* For example, the standing one-arm cable push and pull exercises shown on the following pages teach the body to stabilize against twisting forces, rather than to be twisted by them.

Illustrations

Phase 1.3: Basic Abdominal Exercises

Lower Abdominal Supine Bent Leg

Lower Abdominal Supine Straight Legs

Lower Abdominal Standing Single Leg

Supine Hip Extension on Swiss Ball

Side Flex on Swiss Ball

Reverse Crunch on Swiss Ball

Back Extension on Swiss Ball

Crunch Straight and Oblique on Swiss Ball

Lower Abdominal Supine Bent Leg

Begin by putting your fingers under the low back and tightening your abdominal muscles so the low back presses gently, not tightly, on the fingers. <u>This will be your feedback mechanism</u>: if the pelvis rolls forward, the low back will lift off the fingers, indicating a failure of the lower abdominals to control the pelvis. Start with your knees bent. Raise one leg then lower it, keeping the low back touching the fingers. This is one repetition. In the beginning, you will perform the leg raise with a bent knee.

In this exercise the abdominal muscles, particularly the external obliques, are used to control the pelvis. The pelvis is the foundation of the spine. A stable pelvis is essential to a stable spine.

In many people, the control of the hip flexors, which move the leg off the floor in this exercise, is mixed up with the control of the abdominals, which control the pelvis. So, as the leg lowers, the pelvis wants to follow. The athlete must learn to separate the control of these two muscle groups.

This exercise is progressed by lowering two bent legs simultaneously, as shown in Figure 3. It is further progressed by moving the feet further down until the legs are straight, as shown on the following page.

You can't claim that you have 100% lower abdominal strength until you can do 10 repetitions of the straight leg version of this exercise (next page).

Lower Abdominal Supine Straight Legs

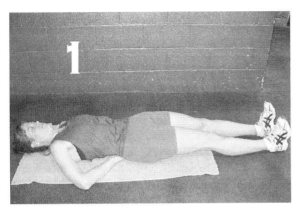

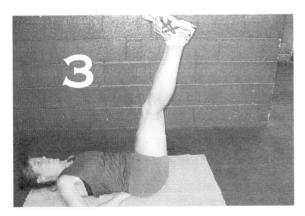

This is a progression of the previous exercise.

As previously, begin by putting your fingers under the low back and tightening the abdominal muscles so the low back presses gently, not tightly, on the fingers. This will be the feedback mechanism. If the pelvis rolls forward, the low back will lift off the fingers. This indicates a failure of the lower abdominals to control the pelvis. Start with knees bent. Raise both legs then lower them, keeping the low back touching the fingers. This is one repetition. In the beginning, you will perform the leg raise with the knees bent.

In this exercise, the abdominal muscles, particularly the external obliques, are used to control the pelvis. The pelvis is the foundation of the spine. A stable pelvis is essential to a stable spine.

In many people, the control of the hip flexors, which move the leg in this exercise, is mixed up with the control of the abdominals which control the pelvis. So, as the leg lowers, the pelvis wants to follow. The athlete must learn to separate the control of these two muscles.

You can't claim 100% lower abdominal strength until you can do 10 repetitions of the straight leg version of this exercise.

Lower Abdominal Standing Single Leg

Begin by putting your fingers under your low back and tightening your abdominal muscles so your low back presses gently on the fingers. It may be difficult to get pressure when standing, because the gluteus muscles hold the low back away from the wall. In this case, just use your fingers to feel if the pelvis rocks forward when the leg moves. This indicates a failure of the lower abdominals to control the pelvis.

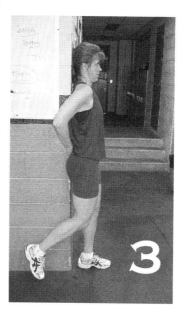

Stand on the corner of a wall. Raise one leg and lower it and raise it a little behind then bring it back to the starting position. This is one repetition.

In this exercise the abdominal muscles, particularly the external obliques, are used to control the pelvis. The pelvis is the foundation of the spine. A stable pelvis is essential to a stable spine.

In many people, the control of the hip flexors, which move the leg in this exercise, is mixed up with the control of the abdominals which control the pelvis. So, as the leg lowers, the pelvis wants to follow. The athlete must learn to separate the control of these two muscles.

Muscularly, this is easier than the supine version of the exercise. But, neurologically speaking, what the body can do lying down it cannot necessarily do standing up. You can use this exercise to transfer the separate control of the pelvis and leg that you learned in the supine position to the standing position.

Supine Hip Extension on Swiss Ball

Begin by resting your shoulder blades on top of the ball with the pelvis down below the knees and knees directly above the ankles. Raise your pelvis until your back, pelvis and thighs are all in a horizontal line. At the same time, keep your shins vertical. Hold for a count of ten. Then lower the pelvis to the starting position. This is one repetition.

This movement exercises the back extensor chain, particularly the gluteus. Be sure to keep a moderate lumbar curve. Occasionally reach back with one of your hands to feel the lumbar spine and check its curvature. Some athletes will tend to flatten their back and others will tend to hyperextend. Both should be moderated. This exercise could be done with the shoulders on the ground, but the Swiss ball adds the element of instability that trains the torso to support the body in integration with the action of the extensors.

Strength in the extensor chain, particularly behind the pelvis, is weakened by the extensive amount of sitting that many students and workers endure. This exercise is an antidote to this aspect of modern life.

This exercise is progressed by doing the movement with one leg extended so it is completely horizontal during the holding phase. Do an equal number of repetitions on each leg. The supine bridge and jack-knife (p.112) are also progressions of the supine hip extension.

Side Flex on Swiss Ball

Begin by bracing your feet against the feet of a training partner while lying with one hip on the ball. (It is possible but more difficult to brace against a wall.) Your upper leg should be in line with your body, while the lower leg reaches forward for balance. Flex sideways, up and away from the ball and then lower down to the starting position. This is one repetition. This exercise should be done an equal number of times on each side.

The two shoulders should always be in a perfectly vertical plane. If you tend to turn your top shoulder forward or back, you are showing a strength imbalance in the oblique abdominals. Concentrate on keeping the shoulders vertical until your body corrects the strength imbalance.

This movement exercises the internal and external obliques on one side of the body as they act in concert to control the forces of side flexion. It is a strength and stability exercise. It does not require speed of motion.

The exercise shown in the photos (with arms behind the head) is made easier by bringing the hands down to cross the chest. It is made more difficult by raising the hands over the head. More advanced forms of this exercise are the standing side flex with a rubber band and the standing side flex toss with a medicine ball.

Reverse Crunch on Swiss Ball

Begin by lying back on the ball and bracing yourself on a piece of equipment that is very heavy or firmly bolted to the floor. You must not be able to pull the equipment over on yourself during the exercise! Raise your legs off of the floor until your pelvis just begins to roll off of the ball. This is the starting position. Now roll the pelvis up toward the ribs. Then lower it back down to touch the ball. This is one repetition.

This motion is the opposite of the straight crunch. The straight crunch pulls the ribs toward the pelvis. The reverse crunch pulls the pelvis towards the ribs. The coordination required by these two exercises is quite different. In the straight crunch the abs are working with the legs as the foundation. In the reverse crunch the abs are working with the arms as stabilizers. This makes the reverse crunch a challenging and refreshing break from crunches with the feet on the ground.

This exercise strengthens the rectus abdominus and prepares it for integrated exercises such as the prone bridges. Also the shoulders must work to keep the body sitting as still as possible on top of the ball. At the same time the obliques must work to keep the pelvis in line with the body which is a bit more mobile due to the fact that it is on a ball. It should be done slowly to give the muscle sufficient time under tension.

Back Extension on Swiss Ball

Begin by lying prone with hips on the ball and feet supported. Some athletes will need to have their feet under a firmly fixed object to avoid tipping over the front of the ball. Get your arms, back and legs into one flat plane. Hold for up to two minutes.

The back extension with arms out, as shown in the photos, is the most difficult version of the exercise. To make the exercise easier, bring the hands back to where they can touch the ears or even further back to cross them over the chest.

Some people will tend to hyperextend their low back while doing this exercise. This is incorrect. The spine should be neutral. It is important to keep the abdominal muscles activated to help control the forward tilt of the pelvis and therefore the hyperextension of the low back. Also the head and neck should be in line with the rest of the spine.

This exercise strengthens the whole back extensor chain but focuses particularly on the spinal erectors. The exercise prepares the body to support the spine in a neutral position for an extended period of light to medium weight stress. If you compare and contrast this exercise with the dead lift you see that they are both exercising the back extensors but this one presents an extended light weight stress whereas the dead lift presents an intermittent heavy weight stress.

This exercise can be progressed by holding small weights such as 2 or 4 pound medicine balls in each hand.

Crunch, Straight and Oblique, on Swiss Ball

Begin by lying back over the ball. Place your tongue against the roof of your mouth (where it lands while swallowing) to fix the sheet of small cervical flexors which will act to roll the head up. Roll the head up. Then crunch up either straight (2) or oblique (3). When doing the oblique crunch do equal numbers to the left and right. Return to the starting position. This is one repetition.

This exercise is superior to crunches off the floor for several reasons. It incorporates the cervical flexors through a larger range of motion, teaching the athlete to control their cranium and thus protect their cervical spine. It exercises the back through a larger range of motion from extension (laying back on the ball) through flexion (crunching forward). And it teaches some side to side stability through the fact that you must control the ball so you don't roll off either side.

This exercise works the front flexor chain and in the oblique form incorporates the oblique abdominals for the purpose of twisting. Adjust the difficulty of the exercise: easier by rolling forward until the ball is under the shoulders; harder by rolling backward until the ball is under the low back. Avoid tilting your head back if you have neck problems or if you experience dizziness.

This exercise can be progressed first by bringing the arms up until the fingers touch the back of the jaw and even more by raising the arms overhead. There is also an accelerated form in which the athlete performs the same crunches pictured here while tossing a medicine ball to a partner.

Phase 2: Integrate!

Combining Individual Muscle Strength into Complex Movements

Phase 2 is called *Integrate!* because it combines the body parts into chains of force. In Phase 2 the athlete practices integrated movements that are closer to sports movements. They transfer energy and movement from one end of the body to the other through the torso. Phase 2 works with lighter weights than Phase 1—sometimes it uses using simple body weight—but it increases complexity and instability.

Traditionally, weight training books such as *The Encyclopedia of Modern Bodybuilding* have shown how to work each muscle separately, giving it a dose of hard work and stimulating it to grow in strength. But does the strength of the individual muscles add up to athletic excellence? Not by itself. *Individual muscles only produce sports success when they work together.* After the individual muscles and their connective tissues have reached a basic level of strength, *learning to integrate the athlete's muscles into useful expressions of force and skill* is the next step in preparing for sports. If you are a fencer (or an athlete with similar athletic needs), and you've reached the basic level, don't simply add ever more weight to your workout— *progress to more complex movements and unstable situations.*

Balanced development is crucial. If a wrestler's arms are strong but his gut and legs are weak, then those strong arms won't push the opponent—they will only push the wrestler's own body backward. In fact, the wrestler's body will sense that the force is going to tear it in half and will "deliberately" weaken the force output of the upper body. The body will refuse to "fire the athlete's cannons" if it senses that those "cannons" are sitting on a canoe! Until the whole body has been built into a "warship," it will constantly try to weaken that wrestler in order to limit the damage to things like knees, lower back and shoulder complex. Sometimes the athlete's willpower may partially overcome the body's protective mechanisms. Then degenerative injury will result.

Each part of the body, all the way down to the ground, must be strong and able to work in coordination with the other parts. It must develop the ability to take force from the ground and transfer it to the hand in a wide variety of ways and circumstances. This is the purpose of *integration* in strength training for fencing.

The exercises in this chapter are not *directly* applicable to fencing. *But this fact does not reduce their importance to the fencer.* They are the crucial next step in developing a supremely capable neuromusculoskeletal machine with which to play at fencing.

Integrated exercises, particularly the cable pulls and pushes, begin to train the various movement systems of the body. These movement systems are groups of muscles that accomplish basic movements found in running, throwing, stepping and lunging. Here is a list of the systems. You can check your anatomy books to map them out. This is not the place for a systematic development of exercises for each movement system. They are mentioned here to show how muscle groups combine in different dimensions and in different basic movements.

1. The Anterior Flexor Chain

Quadriceps, Hip Flexors, Rectus Abdominus, Deep & Surface Cervical Flexors

This system contributes to motions in which the hip flexes, the trunk curls forward and the head tilts forward. So, for example, if you lift both legs and both arms while lying on your back, a whole series of muscles link up, running up and down the front of your body to accomplish this task. If the feet are fixed in position, this chain contributes to the two-handed soccer throw in. When a football player is hit from behind in the lower back, it decelerates the tendency of the chest and head to flop backward. Thus it reduces the whiplash effect of the hit and keeps the athlete from being broken in half. In diving, this muscle chain pulls the athlete into the pike position.

2. The Posterior Extensor Chain
Hamstrings, Gluteus, Spinal Erectors

The posterior extensor chain contributes to motions in which the leg moves backward and the spine bends backward. For example, if you lie on your stomach and lift both legs and both arms there is a series of linked muscles running up and down the back of your body to accomplish this lift. The Aquaman exercise uses this chain. When the planted leg of the runner propels the body forward by pushing backward, the posterior extensor chain does the backward push. In a standing long jump, the posterior extensor chain pushes backward to propel the jumper forward. In various lifting or pulling motions (for example, the squat or the bent over row), it serves to keep the spine from flexing. In the fencing lunge, it keeps the body upright.

3. The Anterior Oblique System
Hip Adductor on One Leg, Same Side Internal Oblique & Opposite Side External Oblique

This system pulls one leg and the opposite shoulder forward at the same time in a motion which brings them towards each other on the diagonal. So, for example, if you lie on your back and lift your right leg and your left arm, a series of muscles link up to run diagonally across the front of your body and accomplish this lift. When you run, the anterior oblique system operates: as one leg drives forward for the next step, the opposite shoulder comes forward also. When the foot is planted, this system contributes to pushing motions such as throwing a ball.

4. The Posterior Oblique System
Gluteus Over One Leg & Opposite Side Latissimus Dorsi

In the first half of a running stride, the anterior oblique system pushes one leg and the opposite shoulder forward. In the second half of the stride, the posterior oblique system pulls them back at the same time in a motion which brings them toward each other on the diagonal and propels the runner forward.

5. The Lateral System
Gluteus Medius and Minimus & Hip Adductors on One Leg;
Quadratus Lumborum & Oblique Abdominals on the Opposite Side

Being able to operate deftly on one leg is an essential ability. The muscles of the lateral system work to hold the pelvis level when one leg (one side of the body's base of support) is lifted to step up or over something. This system is used every time a person walks upstairs or steps into a bathtub. The system is often unevenly weighted, as when a person carries a suitcase up the stairs.

Summary

In the various sports, the muscle chains are called on to do different things to help produce success. Fencing is like other sports in that the ability of the athlete to transmit forces from the feet through the legs and torso is essential. In fencing, however, there is less oblique (twisting) movement than in, for example, swinging a golf club or a baseball bat. The lateral system is used more often in fencing and other martial arts. Recovering from a lunge either forward or back requires great lateral system input—much more than in golf or baseball, where both feet are placed firmly on the ground. On the other hand, martial arts that use kicks employ the lateral system more than sports like fencing or boxing, where the lateral system is mostly used to step from one place to another.

In general, the athlete uses more than one system to accomplish a movement. And at all times, each athlete is using each system in at least a small but essential way. The exercises in Phase 2 take this into account. For example, some of the pushes and pulls are done in a split stance so the pelvis is turned a bit to one side or another. These same pushes and pulls can also be performed with only one leg on the ground, involving yet another system. Either way, they are done with a shoulder turn so that the abdominal muscles learn to deal with changing angles of attack and incorporate the oblique system. Some exercises force the arms to stabilize; others force the legs to stabilize. In summary, the exercises in the integration section are a valuable step towards stronger moves in every sport—including fencing.

2.1 Integrated Pushes, Pulls, and Lunges

Standing Pulls and Pushes with Cable or Rubber Tube

Much of Phase 2 (the Integration Phase) of an athlete's strength training involves strengthening the stabilizer muscles and "educating" the nervous system. This is how the body ties together the power built up in the Separation Phase (Phase 1) in the individual body parts: legs, guts and upper body.

But the athlete may tend to be very shaky when it comes to putting it all together. I have seen high school kids struggle mightily trying to do the standing push exercise on a heavy rubber tube. Their arm and torso flop around because their coordination and stabilizer strength is lacking. These exercises look easy, the kids look weak and uncoordinated. They hate them! But if they have the guts to work through it, they will have a better foundation for good fencing.

When doing the cable exercises (or the same exercises with rubber tubing) the feet stay on the floor, bracing the body, while the torso actively participates in the movement of the hands. This is a lot closer to fencing than lying on a bench and pushing iron up towards the sky. After the body has developed basic strength with Phase 1 exercises like the bench press, the cable exercises take it a step closer to reality. The athlete is in the next phase of improvement.

Athletes will almost invariably be able to push less weight when they start pushing on a cable or tube while standing than they could when pushing weights while lying on a bench. They cannot yet control the twisting, bending and tilting forces— or if they can manage the resistance, they will have resort to poor posture. Their bodies must learn to grab the force from the floor and send it up through the legs, through the torso and out through the hands—all without forcing the spine into a destructive position. All the while, they must maintain good exercise mechanics and belly breathing, while supporting the lower back with their obliques and transverse abdominal muscles.

In Phase 1, you gained experience doing single arm dumbbell bench presses and single arm rows. When you move from lying on the bench to standing pushes, you should revert to a much lower weight until you perfect your form. In a weight room, the standing pushes and pulls can be done with a cable machine. Outside the weight room, you can do standing pushes and pulls with rubber exercise bands. You can work in pairs: one of you anchors the band while the other pushes or pulls.

Beginners should first do the standing pushes and pulls with feet shoulder width, parallel and beside each other. Flexing the knees helps to generate stability.

Once you have mastered form and posture with this position, you can advance to a split stance with one foot somewhat ahead of the other (as though you were ready to begin a foot race, but without leaning over). For all stances, the athlete should exercise both arms.

Complex Lunges

In Phase 1 the athlete mastered the basic weighted lunge. In Phase 2 we take the weight off and add complexity: the walking lunge. Later still, we add small weights by carrying the medicine ball or a dumbbell during the lunge. To do the walking lunge, step forward into the lunge position. Then, rather than stepping backwards out of the lunge to a standing position, bring the back foot forward until it is beside the front foot and you are standing. Then repeat the process, alternating legs and moving across the room. Lunging with hands out to the sides to aid balance is the easiest. Lunging with hands on hips is more challenging. Also try the walking lunge going backwards for a new and rewarding experience. Then progress to doing the walking lunge while holding weights as in Phase 1.

Once you have mastered the walking lunge, you can advance to the lunge with a twist while holding a medicine ball or other weight which is shown in the picture section. Master this exercise with the regular lunge, then progress to the walking lunge with a twist.

The act of combining simple, well-learned motions creates a whole new challenge. The lunge with a twist holding a medicine ball is a particularly fine example, combining an integration challenge with a stability challenge. It integrates movement of the torso (moving a medicine ball from left to right) with the lunge movement. It challenges stability with the weight moving from side to side and changing the center of balance as the exercise progresses. Moving the medicine ball from side to side produces significant lateral forces which tax the lateral muscular system in addition to the systems that work in the basic lunge. Athletes who are adept at the basic lunge will find they are less stable and feel less coordinated when combining upper and lower body motions. Martial arts such as fencing constantly ask athletes to combine upper and lower body skills that they have practiced separately.

Every change presents a learning opportunity for the nervous system. For example, an athlete may be very adept at the walking lunge, but immediately display degraded form when trying to do it backward. To the eye, forward and backward may seem essentially the same because they are mirror images of the same move. But for the body, the backward move is a completely new skill.

Illustrations

Phase 2.1: Integrated Pushes, Pulls, and Lunges

One-Arm Standing Band Push

One-Arm Standing Cable Pull

External Shoulder Rotation Standing With Band

Internal Shoulder Rotation Standing With Band

Lunge With Twist Holding Medicine Ball

Swiss Ball/Medicine Ball Pushup

Inverted Bar Pull on Swiss Ball

One-Arm Standing Band Push

Begin in a square stance, abdominal muscles activated, weighted arm back. Push forward with the weighted arm, then resist the weight as the arm returns to the back position. This is one repetition.

Notice the legs only move a small amount while the arms move a lot. Be sure the unweighted arm moves in the reverse direction.

The rubber band in this picture is anchored to a weight bench out of the picture. In a practice setting this exercise can be done in pairs, one athlete holding the band in their hand to anchor it while their partner performs the exercise.

The external oblique on the pushing side and the internal oblique on the opposite side work in tandem to produce the twisting motion. They are the center of this motion. The athlete should perform an integrated movement, using the legs, the abdominals, the shoulders and arms to get the push.

This exercise can be progressed by doubling the band over or by moving to a heavier rubber band. Performing the exercise in the split stance (one leg or the other placed a little forward and one a little back) provides for a greater range of motion and more twist in the torso. Performing the exercise on one leg is another important progression that challenges whole-body stability.

One-Arm Standing Cable Pull

Begin with feet side by side at shoulder width (parallel stance) or split stance (Photos show the split stance), abdominal muscles activated, weighted arm forward. Pull back with the weighted arm then resist the weight as the arm returns to the forward position. This is one repetition.

The athlete should perform a coordinated movement, using the legs, the belly, the shoulders and arms to get the pull. This sounds easy but most athletes don't get it exactly right the first time. The athlete's first goal will be to get the form right using a light weight. Be sure the unweighted arm moves in the reverse direction.

The cable machine in this picture is set at the lightest setting (20 pounds.) In a practice setting this exercise can be done with rubber tubes in pairs, one athlete holding the band in their hand to anchor it while their partner performs the exercise.

The muscles that power this exercise are the opposite of those in the push: internal oblique on the pulling side and external oblique on the other side. This is an integration exercise. Muscles from the toes up to the shoulders are involved in the pull. It shows how to get power from the floor. Be sure to make the abdominals do a large share of the work.

The balance of this exercise can be changed by performing it in the square stance (shown on p. 89) and by performing it on a single leg.

External Shoulder Rotation Standing with Band

Once athletes have perfected the two free-hand shoulder rotation movements shown on previous pages, they can begin to strengthen specific rotation angles found in fencing. External rotation is found in the prime parry position and the sixte/tierce parry position. In photo A1, the athlete's arm is internally rotated, then, in photo A2, she pulls against the band and externally rotates her arm. In photo B1, the athlete is holding her arm away from her body and internally rotated; then, in photo B2, she pulls against the band and externally rotates her arm. In each exercise position the athlete rotates against the pull of the band and then controls the weight through the release of the rotation. This is one repetition.

There should be no pain. If the athlete experiences pain try to change the position to make the pain stop. If the pain continues stop the exercise until the athlete knows the source of the pain.

The rubber band in this picture is anchored to a weight bench out of the picture. In a practice setting this exercise can be done in pairs, one athlete holding the band in their hand to anchor it while their partner performs the exercise.

There should be no strain in these exercises. Bands are best for shoulder rotation because they are available in smaller weights than are available on cable machines. Start with very light weights and progress the exercise to light weights.

This exercise is a progression of PNF shoulder rotation #1.

Internal Shoulder Rotation Standing with Band

Once athletes have perfected the two free hand shoulder rotation movements shown on previous pages, they can begin to strengthen specific rotation angles found in fencing. Internal rotation is found in the septime (7th) parry position and the quarte (4th) parry position. In photo A1, the athlete begins with her arm externally rotated, then, in photo A2, she pulls against the band and internally rotates her arm. In photo B1, she begins with her arm away from her body and a little externally rotated; then, in photo B2, she pulls against the band and internally rotates her arm. In each exercise position, the athlete rotates against the pull of the band and then controls the weight through the release of the rotation. This is one repetition.

There should be no pain. If the athlete experiences pain, try to change the position to make the pain stop. If the pain continues, stop the exercise until the athlete knows the source of the pain.

The rubber band in this picture is anchored to a weight bench out of the picture. In a practice setting this exercise can be done in pairs, one athlete holding the band in their hand to anchor it while their partner performs the exercise.

There should be no strain in these exercises. Bands are best for shoulder rotation because they are available in smaller weights than are available on cable machines. Start with _very light_ weights and progress the exercise to _light_ weights.

Lunge with Twist Holding Medicine Ball

Once you have perfected the simple lunge exercise, you can progress to the lunge with a twist. Begin standing with the medicine ball held to one side of your body. As you step out into the lunge, move the ball in a semicircle over your head. When you settle in the full lunge, the ball has reached the other side of your body. As you step back out of the lunge, move the ball in the opposite semicircular motion and finish standing where you started. This is one repetition. Keep a vertical upper body and a neutral spine throughout.

This exercise is an integration challenge and a stability challenge. It integrates movement of the torso with the lunge movement. Even without the ball, the lunge is a stability challenge because it is a sort of single leg exercise in that the rear leg (and therefore that whole side of the body) is destabilized by being on the toe. This exercise further challenges stability with the weight moving from side to side and changing the center of balance as the athlete goes through the motion.

The lunge with a twist holding a medicine ball is an advanced form of the lunge exercise. The exercise can be made easier by performing the twist with a smaller ball. As with the basic lunge, the lunge with a twist can be progressed to a walking lunge with a twist and a backward walking lunge with a twist.

Swiss Ball/Medicine Ball Pushup

Begin prone, with feet on a Swiss ball, one hand on a medicine ball and one hand of the floor. Lower your body until the elbows and shoulders are in a line and then push up. This is one repetition. This exercise should be repeated an equal number of repetitions with the medicine ball under the left and right hand.

The balls in this exercise create instability for the torso and the shoulder. This greatly increases the difficulty of a normal pushup because all the muscles that could go to sleep during a regular pushup must now fight to keep the athlete from rolling off of the balls.

The athlete should concentrate on keeping solid abdominals to help the low back. They should also keep good posture in the upper back and head with the chest raised up toward the chin and the head in line with the spine. It is really less than ideal if the athlete accomplishes this exercise by using terrible posture and thus teaches the body to work in a bad position.

This is an advanced integration exercise. A progressed variety of this exercise would be two medicine balls (one for each hand). Have fun but progress with caution. You should not do any exercise where you feel very unstable, as though your shoulder or back could give out without warning and your wrist could slam into the ground. Go back to doing less advanced exercises before trying again.

Inverted Bar Pull on Swiss Ball

Begin by hanging supine on a bar fixed securely on a squat rack with your feet on a Swiss ball. Pull up toward the bar until the elbows and shoulders are in a line. Lower back down. This is one repetition.

Keep a good neutral spine while performing this movement.

This movement integrates the posterior extensor musculature (keeping the body straight from shoulders to heels against gravity, which is trying to make the body sag) with the pulling mechanism of the shoulders (pulling the shoulder blades toward the spine and pulling the upper arms toward the shoulder blades) and also with the oblique musculature (keeping the body from twisting and rolling off the Swiss ball.)

This exercise is similar to the bent over row. In the bent over row the athlete moves the hands toward the body. In the inverted bar pull the athlete pulls the body toward the hands. In the bar pull there is the added element of instability caused by the Swiss ball.

There is an advanced form of this exercise that progresses the stress on the oblique musculature about tenfold. In the progressed form the athlete begins as described then releases the bar with one hand, pulls with the other arm and punches up above the bar with the free hand. (No one in my group could perform it but it is possible!)

2.2 Balance Challenges

Stability and Balance: Training in Unstable Situations

We began balance training in the beginning of Phase I with the single leg stand. Instability is really a Phase 2 form of overload, but the single leg stand is too important a form of protection for any athlete's legs and low back. It had to be practiced and perfected early. Now we come to other forms of balance and stability.

There are two types of human physical instability, and therefore two types of balance exercise. The difference is in the condition of the athlete's base (point or points of support):

Two types of instability

1. The part of the athlete above the base is jostled or unbalanced, while the athlete's base is *fixed*.
2. The part of the athlete above the base is jostled or unbalanced, while the athlete's base is *slipping (or sometimes flying, but fencers don't fly very far, even when fleching!)*

Fixed foot/unstable upper body exercises—the first category—include every exercise where athletes are on one or both feet and their limbs and/or body are in motion in any direction, whether the motion is free or the result of being pushed or pulled. There are countless examples in sports: golfing, martial arts, football. Even if the athlete moves from one fixed position to another—think of a runner—he or she is employing fixed foot balance.

The second category, in which the base is slipping, includes sports such as ice skating, skiing, surfing, and skate boarding. It wouldn't make any sense for an ice hockey player to say, "Boy, that playing surface is slippery!" Of course it's slippery: hockey is a game of controlled slipping. In fencing, on the other hand, a complaint that the floor is slippery makes sense and requires attention.

There are some sports which we might consider hybrids of fixed and slipping balance. In platform diving a diver exercises fixed foot balance while standing on their toes at the edge of a precipice and then slipping (or really, "flying") as they perform highly controlled stunts while flying through the air. The same can be said of the floor exercises in gymnastics, where the athlete must perform precarious one-legged stands at one moment and at the next moment perform precise movements in the air.

In fencing, upper body unbalance/fixed feet predominates. Foot slippage occurs mostly as an accident. The first priority for fencers is fixed-base stability. The fixed-base balance exercises in this book (for example, those on pages 102, 103, 104, and 129) increase sports accuracy and the transmission of strength through the limbs. They are also very important for injury prevention because they stabilize the low back, neck and shoulders in the perfect position of power. The athlete's first task in regard to stability is to be strict about posture and exercise form while doing every exercise from basic squats to explosive jump lunges.

The general methods of adding instability to an exercise are as follows:

- narrow the base of support,
- soften (or otherwise destabilize) the footing,
- put forces into the athlete's body which tend to unbalance it (these forces are called "perturbations" by physical therapists),
- reduce the role of vision in the athlete's balance.

The athlete and coach accomplish these general methods with specific combinations of techniques and tools. The most important of these combinations are listed below.

1. *The foam pad:* The foam pad is the centerpiece of modern instability training. I recommend the Airex pad—it's mushy, but not too mushy, and there's a more expensive model with a sticky bottom. For a freely available substitute, use a pillow.

Foam pad

> **Be careful that the pad or pillow doesn't slip and that you have something firm to grab onto if your balance is bad enough that you start to topple over. Don't be embarrassed. Be safe.**

You may be one of those people who, like me, have bad equilibrium. When I close my eyes while doing a one-leg stand on a Airex pad all hell breaks loose and I struggle mightily to stay up. I almost always have to resort to grabbing the back of a chair before my time is up.

> **Airex pads do slip. All physical therapy establishments use Airex pads over a piece of that rubberized netting that's sold for use under throw rugs. So should you.**

After mastering the one-legged stand described in the section on posture (3 sets of 30 seconds on each leg) you should progress the exercise by doing the stand on a foam pad. This is a big progression because of the intense destabilizing effect of the pad. After you have mastered the pad, you can progress to the one-legged stand on the pad with your eyes closed.

2   *The balance beam:* The beam can be as simple as a pair of 1 inch by 4 inch by 8 feet long pine boards screwed together. This device is used with the four inch side flat on the floor. (This may sound a lot like a 2x4, but I consider a 2x4 a poor substitute because it has rounded edges, so the beam can roll too easily. In addition, a 2x4 is sold with a high moisture content so it tends to warp.)

Balance beam

In the most basic balance beam exercise, you walk forward and backward on the beam touching your heel to your toe as you go. This gives you a small and narrow base. You can advance this exercise by walking with your eyes closed.

3. *The medicine ball:* The medicine ball is used to teach athletes to stabilize themselves against incoming forces. You must dampen the forces of the medicine ball both as it comes into the body and, just as important, as you throw it back again. The medicine ball is unique in being able to provide large amplitude forces at all angles, including twisting.

Medicine ball

After mastering the one-legged stand described previously (3 sets of 30 seconds on each leg) you can progress the exercise by tossing and catching a medicine ball while standing on one leg. A still more advanced version of this toss and catch is to make the toss out to the side of the athlete's body so that some of the ball's force tends to twist the athlete.

Next, after mastering the one-legged toss and catch (3 sets of 10 catches on each leg), you can progress the exercise again by doing the toss and catch *while standing one-legged on the foam pad.* This is a big jump in difficulty.

For some reason unknown to me, this exercise was considered tremendous fun by some of my better athletes. They devised a game where the challenge was to take off their sweatshirt, T-shirt, breakaway sweatpants, one sock and one shoe— one at a time, of course, while standing on one leg on the Airex pad— and then put them all back on. I still smile when I think of those knuckleheads. But in all seriousness, a coach should never prescribe something that goes further than the athlete dressed in common athletic attire, which is short pants and T-shirt.

Swiss ball

4.   *The Swiss ball:* The Swiss ball is an absolutely necessary tool for abdominal training as described below. It can also be used to add instability to common weightlifting and strengthening exercises. For example, after mastering the double and single arm versions of the dumbbell bench press, the athlete can progress the exercise by doing double and single arm bench presses lying back on the Swiss ball with the feet flat on the floor and the shins perpendicular to the floor. *This greatly increases the difficulty of the exercise and should be started with very light weights.* Another example is the common pushup. After mastering the pushup while keeping a good lumbar and thoracic curve during the exercise, athletes can progress the exercise by performing the pushup with the feet resting on a Swiss ball.

Cable/Rubber band

5.   *The cable or rubber band*: The strength training athlete should progress from the regular standing cable push and pull to doing the same exercises on one leg. *The single leg version should be done with very light weights to start and only after the two leg versions have been mastered.* So, which leg should you stand on? The easiest and most valuable one-leg stance is to stand on the leg opposite the weighted hand. (If the cable handle is in your right hand, you should be standing on your left leg.) Another option is to perform the push or pull on a single leg directly under the weighted hand. (If the cable is in your right hand, you should be standing on your right leg.) The final challenge is to do a one-legged push or pull while standing on a foam pad. Is there no end to the fun?

The lower body instability exercises can be used both to provoke the nervous systems of highly athletic people to greater performance and to stimulate people with "sleepy" nervous systems. Not all people are endowed with first class nervous systems, but some have a fairly good one that has fallen asleep after years of disuse. One technique that rehabilitation experts use to wake up these nervous systems is to put the person in a situation that their brain interprets as dangerous. Then the brain thinks, "We're going to fall!" and sends an emergency call to nerves that haven't been used in years. Exercises to use include single leg exercises, exercises standing on a foam pad, and pushups with feet on the Swiss ball.

Stability exercises can decrease injuries by 80% – 90% in previously injured athletes.

Stability exercises improve the athlete's reaction to unstable situations. Mastering them has been shown to decrease the incidence of injury by 80 – 90%. This is particularly important for athletes who have had a previous injury. When an athlete tears a ligament and the doctor replaces it, the athlete has reduced proprioceptive sense and is more likely to suffer another injury. The ligaments and tendons are sensory organs (mechanoreceptors) as well as mechanical restraints, and they have to relearn their stabilizing role after an injury.

Mastering of stability exercises also increases accuracy and performance. Scientists and clinicians surmise that both effects—reduced injury and increased accuracy—result from some form of proprioceptive, kinesthetic, or somatosensory awareness. (*Proprioception* refers to the body's internal perception of where it is. *Kinesthetic awareness* is our sense of movement. *Somatosensory awareness* includes all of the body's senses, a sort of grand sum of proprioception, kinesthetic awareness, the traditional five external senses, and various kinds of organ awareness.). There are scientific arguments concerning which of these three big words—or what combination of them—best describes why these benefits occur. However, for practical purposes, we can say the stability exercises improve the athlete's sense of where the body is and where it is going. Thus they improve the ability to avoid injury and successfully execute athletic movements.

The body awareness that is developed through mastery of balance exercises becomes a multifaceted tool for the athlete. Balance affects both *stable* situations (for example, planting a foot, stopping, extending the arm from en garde) and *dynamic* situations (for example, keeping the center of balance over the feet during advances, retreats, changes of direction, and lunges, as well as recovery of balance after unbalanced actions like fleches, "flunges," one-legged leaning stop hits, etc.) Balance may be *consciously* mediated, as when an athlete works to change the position of a limb in a given sports move (think of extending both front and rear arms in a lunge). It may also be *unconsciously* mediated, as when the body senses that a joint is moving out of position and reflexively tightens muscles to protect it.

> **Repeated short exposure to various balance and stability exercises is better than long grueling practice sessions. The body is quick to adapt to somatosensory input.**

For an example of how quickly the body adapts, suppose I ask you to lift ten cardboard boxes from the floor to a shelf. Most people will use somatosensory perception and "learn" the tension of back and arm muscles necessary to lift the first nine boxes. But what I didn't tell you was that, while the first nine boxes weighed ten pounds each, the last box weighs only one pound. You will probably use that learned method on the last, light box and pull much too hard on it. In other words, it only took you nine repetitions to learn the "right" effort. So in general, balance exercise sessions don't need to be grueling, hour-long affairs. Five or ten minutes of balance exercise at a time is plenty.

Five or 10 minutes of balance exercises at a time—that's plenty!

Illustrations

Phase 2.2: Balance Challenges

Dumbbell Bench Press on Swiss Ball

Single-Leg Medicine Ball Toss and Catch

Single-Arm Single-Leg Band Pull

Balance Beam Tandem Walk with Medicine Ball

Reach-up Pushup on Medicine Ball

Pushup with One Arm on a Foam Block

Dumbbell Bench Press on Swiss Ball

Begin with your shoulder blades on the ball and shoulders, knees and hips in a horizontal line. Receive the weights from a coach or training partner. Lower the weights keeping forearms vertical. This is the beginning position. Push the weights toward the ceiling and lower them to the beginning position. This is one repetition.

This motion exercises the front part of the shoulder in a pushing motion while adding the need to stabilize the torso against rolling off the ball and the shoulders against any minor changes in torso position. You should be able to keep a very steady position on top of the ball. If you are flopping around on the ball while you are trying to lift the weights, you should decrease the weights or go back to doing the supine hip extension until you develop more stability.

The dumbbell bench press on the Swiss ball is a progression of the simple bench press. You should begin with less weight than you used on the bench. Notice that you are also doing the supine hip extension on the Swiss ball, so this should be considered a prerequisite as well.

This exercise can be progressed by adding weight as well as moving the weights alternately and working with a single weight in one hand. It is also related to the standing one-arm pushes.

Single-Leg Medicine Ball Toss and Catch

> **This exercise is an essential part of an injury prevention program.**

Begin by standing on one leg. The coach or training partner tosses a softball size medicine ball. You catch it with one hand, stabilize, and toss the ball back. Your partner will toss to one side or the other, high or low and even over the head at random. You should perform an equal number of catches on each leg. Two training partners can exercise simultaneously, each standing on one leg and tossing back and forth.

This motion exercises balance and stability, particularly the lateral system and the stabilizers of the knee and ankle. To train endurance of the stability muscles, progress to 3 sets of 15 tosses with each leg.

A prerequisite to this exercise is the single leg stand in all its variations. The single leg toss and catch is progressed by moving from a 2 pound ball to a 4 and then even a 6 pound ball, depending on the size and strength of the athlete. A throw close to the body is easier to catch and balance because the weight stays close to the center of gravity. The training partner can increase the challenge by tossing the ball so the athlete must fully extend their arm to catch it. In the final progression of the exercise the athlete tosses and catches while standing on one leg on a foam pad.

Single-Arm Single-Leg Band Pull

Begin by standing on one leg. Hold a band or a weight cable in the hand opposite the leg you are standing on. Pull the weight back, being sure to incorporate the abdominals into the motion. At the end of the pull the elbow should be in the same plane as the two shoulders and the upper back. The unweighted hand should be moving in the opposite direction from the weighted hand at all times. Release the weighted hand back to the forward position. This is one repetition.

This exercise can be done alternately by two partners, each taking a turn anchoring the band.

This motion exercises balance. It also exercises the lateral system (any time the body is on one leg the lateral system is at work), the knee and the ankle. It has an oblique component in that the motion involves twisting. It also has a dynamic component in that it teaches stability of the spine while moving a weight. This exercise works well as part of a balance training circuit; for example, one set each of one-arm one-leg pull, one-leg stand on pad with eyes closed and side to side bound to single leg stand.

A prerequisite to this exercise is the one arm push and pull while standing on two legs. The one arm one leg variety is progressed by increasing the weight of the band. It is also progressed by standing on the leg directly under the weighted hand. It is further progressed by standing with either leg on a foam pad.

Balance Beam Tandem Walk with Medicine Ball

Begin with your feet on the balance beam, front heel touching rear toe. The medicine ball is held off to one side. Place your rear foot in front of your front foot and move the medicine ball to the other side of the body. Do not look at the feet or the beam. Look forward. Continue placing one foot directly in front of the other and moving the medicine ball to the opposite side with each step. Move to the far end of the balance beam. Then return going backward.

The apparatus pictured is a very simple homemade balance beam. It is made by screwing together two 1" x 4" x 8' pine boards, then giving them a couple of coats of polyurethane.

This is a balance exercise. It is very much a somatosensory exercise, teaching the athlete's body to feel the position of their limbs and adjust and stabilize. Fixing the eyes on an object somewhere beyond the end of the beam makes the athlete more stable. This exercise can also be done in all its forms by pacing sideways down the beam and back.

This exercise is made easier by performing it without the ball. It is progressed by focusing on the ball and turning the head to follow the ball. This largely removes the eyes from the balance function and puts all the pressure on the somatosensory system in the legs and torso.

Reach-up Pushup on Medicine Ball

Begin on the floor in the pushup position with a medicine ball near one hand. Put one hand on the medicine ball and raise up into a one-armed pushup position with the other arm out to the side. Turn the whole torso until your arms form a single line from the top of the medicine ball toward the ceiling. Return to the arm out to the side position and then to both hands down. The is one repetition. This exercise should be performed an equal number of times with each arm.

Perform this exercise with perfect posture of the hips, spine and head just like the position that was learned in the 4-point stance superman. The stress of this difficult exercise will push many athletes into poor posture. Practice patiently until your body learns the perfect position.

The athlete should have mastered the cobra, the pushup extension, the bench press and the pushup before they attempt this exercise. This exercise is very challenging to the abdominals and to the strength of the one arm that supports the body. Also the muscles of the shoulder and arm must stabilize the ball. The muscles of the hips and torso must stabilize the body which is experiencing twisting force because of the loss of one of its supports (the raised arm).

This exercise can be made easier by performing it on the floor without the medicine ball under the hand. This easier version makes a good group training exercise.

Pushup with One Arm on a Foam Block

Begin in the pushup position with one arm on a foam yoga block. Lower your body until the elbows and shoulders are in a line. Return to the beginning position. This is one repetition. This exercise should be done an equal number of times with the block under each arm for balanced development.

This is an advanced pushup exercise. The athlete should have mastered the cobra, the pushup extension, the bench press and the pushup before they attempt this exercise.

This motion exercises the shoulder and teaches it to stabilize under the influence of forces that are coming from a different angle. The point is to teach the athlete's body to keep the shoulders in a strong and stable position even when circumstances are a little off-center. It should be considered a strength and stability exercise. Therefore, control and form are essential and speed is unnecessary. Keep the back, hips, head and chest in a good position just like the position learned in the 4-point stance superman.

This exercise can be progressed by performing it with the hand on a medicine ball rather than a yoga block. The athlete can roll the medicine ball from hand to hand as they alternate raised arms.

2.3 Integrated Abdominal Exercises

In all the exercises that we do, the abdominal muscles provide stability for the spine and transfer of force from one end of the body to the other. So in a very practical way, *all integrated exercises are abdominal exercises:* they use the center of the body to carry forces from feet to hands and from hands to feet. This integration of the whole body is the key to Phase 2 abdominal exercises.

Integrated abdominal exercises are classified according to the forces that they stabilize against—whether they try to twist you around or bend you forward, backward, or sideways. These feats of stabilization use one or more of the chains of muscles mentioned earlier. The athlete should develop all these skills.

Many integrated abdominal exercises utilize the Swiss ball (for example, those on pages 110-112). In these exercises, the athlete lies on the Swiss ball prone or supine (face down or face up). Either the shoulder area rests on the ball and the feet on the ground or vice versa. The force of gravity will attempt to bend or twist the athlete, who must strive for a stable posture.

Let's say you are trying to do a pushup on the Swiss ball. You are facing the ground with your feet on the ball and your hands on the floor. The force of gravity is trying to bend your spine backward (extension), while the ball itself is trying to roll out from under you. In this way, the Swiss ball, by providing a complex multidirectional force to contend with, makes your body much smarter.

> **Avoid weighted exercises with extension or flexion of the spine (bending it backward or forward). They are rarely beneficial and usually dangerous.**

Excessive flexion of the spine (bending forward) under weight can force the discs toward the nerves of the spine and cause pain. Hyper-extension (bending backward) can also cause pain and in the long run can cause wear and tear. The spine itself has 40 degrees of extension built into it. So it is not unnatural to do unweighted flexibility exercises such as the abdominal crunch over the Swiss ball where the spine goes backward past straight and into extension. Generally speaking abdominal exercises have the athlete doing flexion and extension. But don't forget that the position of power in the body is a neutral spine. The body isn't built to handle great stress in extremes of spinal flexion or extension.

> **Get advice from a doctor if you have a disc injury. Even if you are healthy, be sure to master the exercises in the order they are presented, phase by phase.**

Notice that there is a difference between rotational movement and rotational forces in an exercise. The rotational forces in exercises such as Supine Lateral Swiss ball Roll can potentially twist an athlete's body. But in doing the exercise, the athlete resists the twisting forces, maintains a neutral spine throughout the exercise and learns to stabilize the spine against twisting forces. In an exercise such as the Supine Swiss ball Drop and Punch, the athlete does actual rotational motion but it is controlled, it has a limit. In the Drop and Punch, the athlete learns to limit the distance and control the extent of rotation by using the abdominal muscles. If you have a disc injury you should discuss this information with your doctor.

> **All these exercises should be pain free for all athletes. If you experience pain while doing any exercise, immediately discontinue the exercise until you know the source of the pain.**

It is possible to limit the range of motion, whether it is flexion, extension, or twisting, and still gain fitness from controlled force exercises. Limited-motion or static exercises benefit healthy people as well, so don't ignore them just because you have no injury.

For people with previous injuries, controlled-force exercises can serve as recovery exercises. For people without injuries, they can serve as preventive exercises. They may not be the most exciting exercises you can perform, but they are exceedingly valuable.

Illustrations

Phase 2.3: Integrated Abdominal Exercises

Prone Swiss Ball Bridge / Jacknife Pike (Pushup Position)

Supine Lateral Swiss Ball Roll

Supine Swiss Ball Bridge / Jacknife

Standing Side Flex with Rubber Band

Metronome Twist on Swiss Ball

Ball Hug Twist on Swiss Ball

Cable Wood Chop

Prone Swiss Ball Bridge/Jackknife/Pike

Begin in the pushup position with shins on top of the ball as in photo 1. Have a neutral spine and activated abdominals. This is a stability exercise called the prone bridge. The most common mistake will be to overuse the rectus abdominus and flex the spine forward. Work your way up to holding this position for two minutes.

From the bridge, progress to the jackknife, where you pull your knees in and roll the ball forward as in Photo 2. After flexing the knees, return to the bridge and a good neutral spine. This is one repetition.

From the jackknife, progress to the pike. Start in the bridge position. Flex at the hips and bring the feet towards the head as in photo 3. Return to the bridge position and a good neutral spine. This is a strenuous exercise. Take it slow.

These motions exercise stability and coordination in the spine and shoulders. They utilize the anterior flexor chain in a stabilizing capacity while integrating shoulder function to support the body on the arms. These motions should be done in a slow and controlled manner, teaching the body how to maintain good form under stress.

For these exercises the athlete should be proficient in the pushup extension shown in the section on posture exercises (p. 48).

Supine Lateral Swiss Ball Roll

In this exercise, a rod the length of the outstretched arms is used to indicate clearly the position of the shoulders and hips.

Begin supine, feet on the floor and shoulder blades on the ball. Hold the rod across your shoulders from hand to hand. Roll the ball to the right (you can move your feet) so that your right shoulder blade starts to go off the ball. Hold for 3 seconds. (Photo #2) Roll back to the center. Roll the ball to your right so that the left shoulder blade starts to go off the ball. Hold for 3 seconds. Roll back to the center. This is one repetition.

The rod should always be horizontal. The shoulders should be in a horizontal line beneath it. The hips should remain in the same plane as the shoulders. Some athletes will tend to twist (hips go one way, shoulders go the other) as they get off the ball, others will sink on one side. Take the time to teach the body to feel the correct position and not cheat to support the overhanging shoulder.

This motion teaches the body to stabilize against twisting forces (turning the unsupported shoulder down) and against flexing forces (pulling the pelvis toward the floor). It is a tough exercise to do well and takes time to learn. When you have learned this exercise, you have accomplished a lot.

If an intermediate to advanced athlete doesn't have much time to spend in a workout, this exercise would accomplish much in a short period of time.

This exercise is progressed to a dynamic form called the Drop and Punch Up.

Supine Swiss Ball Bridge/Jackknife

Begin the bridge portion of this exercise lying on your back with your ankles on top of the ball. Then raise your pelvis until it is in a straight line with your ankles and shoulders, as shown in Photo 1. At this point you should have a good neutral spine. Hold for a count of ten and lower to the ground. This is one repetition of the bridge. The bridge can be progressed by using only one leg at a time to raise the torso off the ground.

In the jackknife version of this exercise, begin in the bridge position (hips off of the ground). Then pull your ankles in towards your hips as in Photo 2. Then go back to the bridge position. Keep a perfect neutral spine throughout. This is one repetition. The jackknife can be progressed by using one leg at a time.

This exercise works the posterior extensor chain. When it is done with one leg there is also significant oblique (twisting) work. This exercise is used to develop strength, integration and stability. Therefore it should be done at a medium to slow speed with great attention to form.

Some athletes may need to develop proficiency in the supine hip extension before they can accomplish the supine bridge and jackknife. The bridge and jackknife put more tension into the hamstring than the hip extension exercise.

112

Standing Side Flex with Rubber Band

Begin with hands overhead, grasping the band which is anchored off to one side about head high. In the photo the band is doubled over and the athlete is grasping both handles. In the standing upright position the band is stretched a little bit. Thus the exercise begins under tension and continues under tension for the duration of the exercise. Flex sideways against the pull of the band, keeping the shoulders and hips in one plane (no twisting). Stand upright again. This is one repetition. It should be repeated an equal number on both sides.

This motion exercises the oblique abdominals on one side of the body in integration with the arms and legs. In side flexion the internal and external oblique on one side of the body pull together to bend the body sideways. These same muscles produce a twist when fired on opposite sides of the body. For example, firing the internal oblique on the right side and the external oblique on the left produces a twist to the right.

This exercise is like the side flex on Swiss ball. The standing version of the exercise might be considered a progression of the Swiss ball version because it integrates the legs, hips and arms with the action of the side flexors. A progression of this exercise is the standing side flex medicine ball toss and catch.

Metronome Twist on Swiss Ball

Begin in the supine hip extension position, with hands reaching toward the ceiling holding a medicine ball. Turn your shoulders to one side while keeping the ball out in front of your chest. Bring your shoulders back to horizontal and turn them to the other side, carrying the ball out in front of your chest. Return to lying with your back flat on the ball and your arms reaching the ball toward the ceiling. This is one repetition.

The action imitates the arm of a metronome as it swings back and forth to keep time for a practicing musician. The knees, pelvis, shoulders and head top should be kept in a horizontal line. Some minor twisting of the pelvis in the direction of the shoulder turn may occur. Keep good posture and activated abdominals.

This motion exercises the oblique musculature of the torso in an unstable situation. It also integrates the twisting motion with the need to extend the hips.

This is a challenging abdominal exercise. The athlete should have a solid background of basic abdominal exercises.

This exercise can be made easier by using a lighter ball and harder by using a heavier ball. Speed is not important in this exercise.

Ball Hug Twist on Swiss Ball

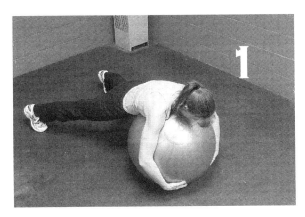

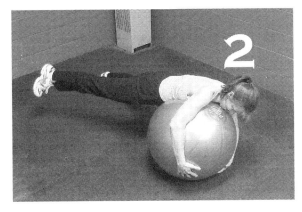

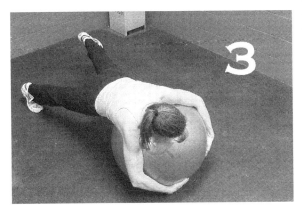

Begin prone, feet on the floor and chest on the ball. Grasp the ball with both arms. Reach your hands forward toward your head a bit so that they don't get caught underneath the ball as it rolls. Roll the ball to the left until you feel you are about to tip over. The foot away from the direction of lean may raise off the ground. Hold one second. Roll across to the right until you feel you are about to tip over. Hold one second. Return to the starting position. This is one repetition.

There is a lot of twisting force going into the one toe that is on the ground. On the way to the toe, the force is going through the knee. Don't overdo it and strain the knees. Once the foot comes up stop going in the direction you are going and return towards the center. Moderate the force if necessary by not rolling over as far. Keep a good neutral spine and activated abdominals. The athlete should not side flex or hyperextend during the exercise.

The motion works the oblique system to control the twisting forces. It also involves a bit of side flexion control and extension control. This is a stability exercise, so medium to slow speed is fine.

This exercise is progressed in the twisting ball throw exercises such as Standing Twist Medicine Ball Toss.

Cable Wood Chop

Begin with your right side toward the machine so the cable can be pulled across the front of your body. First grasp the handle of the cable with your left hand. Then put your right hand over top of your left hand. Turn to the left, pulling the weight across your body and down, in a twisting motion. Return to the beginning position. This is one repetition. The exercise should be repeated an equal number of times on each side.

In the photo the anchor point is above the athlete's head so the pull goes in a downward position. The anchor point can also be level with the hands in which case the pull would be perfectly level. When the exercise is performed on the level, it is called a Standing Twist rather than a Wood Chop.

The exercise works the oblique system. In the bottom photo, the athlete is looking down to help herself concentrate on using her left internal oblique. As she gets better at the exercise, the coach will encourage her to keep her head up and looking forward as though at an opponent. There should be no side or forward flexion in the movement. As the athlete gets tired, the body will begin to add muscles that cause side and forward flexion to try to help the tired obliques. <u>This means it is time to stop the set</u>. When using the rubber band be sure to anchor it safely.

This is a strengthening and integrating exercise. It uses the obliques integrated with the arms and legs. Speed is not important.

This exercise can be performed with bands instead of a cable machine.

Phase 3: Accelerate!
Developing Explosive Strength

Phase 3 is called *Accelerate* because its exercises accelerate the body quickly from a standstill and decelerate it quickly from motion. Phase 3 movements are closer to sports movements than those of the previous two phases: they are springy, quick, explosive, or involve heavy deceleration. *This phase works with lighter weights,* sometimes using simple body weight, and, as we have said, increases the factors of acceleration and deceleration, complexity and instability.

Some older coaches and athletes will be amused at the irony of calling a strength-training program "modern" when it includes medicine ball exercises. When I was a kid, the leader of our fencing club in New Brunswick was a wonderful old Hungarian gentleman named Frank Farkas. (He insisted that we call him Uncle Frank in Hungarian: it sounded like "Ferry Batchee.") Let me take a moment to acknowledge him. He was a man of unheralded greatness, an example of dignity, dedication, and caring. Anyway, Mr. Farkas would exercise with this beat-up old leather medicine ball, tossing it and swinging it. We looked at him like he was crazy, wondering why he didn't use iron weights like Arnold! It turns out he was just so far behind the times that he had gotten ahead of them. Medicine balls are old, but they have become new again.

When the speed of an exercise is increased, the forces on the athlete's body increase. When the athlete graduates to the point of accelerating through a motion—that is, they constantly increase speed throughout the whole motion, the forces increase greatly. These accelerated motions are often loosely called plyometrics. The word "plyometrics" itself refers to the ballistic use of change of direction. And the science of plyometrics packs as much use of ballistic change of direction as possible into each exercise. But life is ballistic, too, just not quite as concentrated ballistic as a plyometric routine. *Whenever you do something "as fast as possible,"* even if it is simply running or doing simple fencing footwork, *you are doing an advanced exercise with respect to bodily strength because you are using more acceleration and deceleration.* Athletes need a solid background in the slower exercises before they are adequately prepared to do the fast exercises. Slow exercise is particularly necessary for the strengthening of the connective tissue, which is put under high tension during high acceleration.

After the basics of accelerating exercise are mastered, the coach and athlete can try to be more experimental and creative in making the exercises more closely match the motions of fencing. Coaching guru Kim Goss, in an article on the misuse of plyometrics, noted that plyometric exercises are often practiced in ways that are simply the opposite of the neuromechanics of the sport. As an example, he pointed out that figure skaters do most of their jumps off one leg while skating backwards. But in standard plyometrics, they would jump off two legs forward and up onto a box. They could make their strength training more applicable to their sport by simply turning around and doing the same jump "backwards."

I have tried to follow Coach Goss's principle and keep the exercises in this section applicable to fencing. They have been selected from hundreds of exercises because of their similarity to fencing mechanics or their value in developing a the fencer's body. Thus, for example, we will be using few vertical jumps, which are not very important in fencing, and more horizontal jumps (which are). Certainly fencers do many moves that are like shuttle runs (running sideways in such a way that the feet do not cross), lunges, hops (short jumps where the feet leave the ground

Phase 3 movements are closer to sports movements. They use less resistance.

Before starting Phase 3, an athlete needs a background in slower exercises.

The exercises in this section have been selected for their relevance to fencing.

117

and land together) and bounds (longer jumps where the athlete takes off on one leg and lands on the other).

When you get too tired, you train yourself to be slow.

A common mistake occurs when fatigue is allowed to ruin the speed training aspect of acceleration exercises. When athletes get too tired, they train themselves to be slow. Accelerated exercises are not aerobic exercises. One continuous period (say a minute) of blazing, muscle-burning speed is much better for speed training than two or three minutes of slowly diminishing performance.

Let me take a moment to explain. As mentioned earlier, two energy systems come into play in sports: one slow and one fast. The athlete in training must understand that the duration of an exercise determines which energy system will be worked and therefore determines the intensity of the exercise. If the exercise lasts longer than one minute, it goes well past the endurance of the fast energy system and it cannot be performed at maximum speed. Therefore if your purpose is to train maximum speed, then after one minute (at most) you must stop, rest and recover. Even one minute is too long! In an extreme speed sport such as the 100 meter dash, maximum speed begins to diminish about halfway through the race: during the last fifty yards, the runners are trying to maintain form. The *most extreme speed* lasts for less than five seconds. So why do I say that the plyometric exercise set begins to drop off after a minute? Because the expression of speed is sport-specific. The leg speed that you can get from the 10th to the 60th second of plyometric exercise may be sufficient for a great epeeist but not a great 100 meter sprinter.

Cycle through a variety of speeds and exercises to avoid overload.

Athletes should not practice one speed or pattern of motion day in and day out. Otherwise they may develop what is called pattern overload—that is, the fibers of the body that are most strained by a particular pattern of motion become over-worked and begin to weaken. Just three straight weeks of high speed training with a few exercises can lead to this. It is more likely in an athlete who works only on weight machines because machines restrict the body to the exact same pattern on every repetition. But it happens in other situations as well. *The athlete should cycle a variety of speeds and exercises to avoid pattern overload.*

Table 3: The Three Energy Systems

Fast Energy System	**Medium Energy System**	**Slow Energy System**
Energy Reserves for 15 seconds of work	Energy Reserves for 2 minutes of work	Energy Reserves for hours of work
High Strength	Moderate Strength	Lower Strength
High Speed	Moderate Speed	Lower Speed
Poor Endurance	Moderate Endurance	High Endurance
This is the *anaerobic energy system.* It burns adenosine triphosphate supplied by the Medium Energy System, which manufactures it from creatine phosphate.	This is the *lactic energy system.* It burns creatine phosphate. It is fed by the fat and carbohydrates of the slow energy system.	This is the *aerobic energy system.* It burns fat and carbohydrates supplied by the digestive system, which makes them out of the food we eat.

Work

Food Air Water

1. Accelerating Leg Motions

Jumps

Each plyometric jump is related to one of the leg exercises from Phase 1: the squat and the lunge. The athlete should have a firm foundation in these weight-lifting exercises before advancing to the jumps. The jumps related to the lunge, such as the jump lunge and the step-up jump, tend to be single-leg oriented and have more extreme hip flexion. The squat-related jumps could use one or two legs and stress jumping distances either side to side, up and down or forward and back (rather than stressing extremes of leg position like the lunge). Examples of the squat related jumps are the *box jump*, the *lateral bound* and the *dot drill*.

(If you are wondering what happened to the calf raise from Phase 1, the calf muscle was integrated into top to bottom exercises like the cable pull and push. In the same way there is no Phase 2 of the rhomboid exercise (cobra) or serratus anterior (pushup extension). They are secondary/supporting muscles and as such melt into the big picture after Phase 1.)

Plyometric jumps are also categorized by difficulty. In order from least difficult to most difficult, the categories are called *level jump*, *box jump* and *depth jump*.

In *level jumps*, the athlete begins and ends on the same level or at the same altitude. This includes jumping up and down in place, jumping back and forth or side to side and jumping repeatedly in the same direction to get from one place to another across a level floor. *Level jumps*

In *box jumps*, the athlete goes from a lower level to a higher level and back. They are called box jumps because the athlete usually jumps onto a hefty box-like piece of equipment. Stadium steps are also useful for this purpose. The step-up jump is another box jump. It may be thought of as the box version of the lunge because of the position of the hip and knee of the leg that has stepped up onto the box. *Box jumps*

The *depth jump* is the opposite of a box jump: The athlete jumps down from a box to the floor, gathers all the energy from the downward momentum, lets all the tendons in the leg stretch and absorb the falling energy, and, after a momentary contact with the floor, jumps upward as high as possible. The extreme forces generated in this action are especially taxing for the connective tissues. It should be treated like a heavy lift and done in sets composed of a very low number of repetitions interspersed with rest periods. *Depth jumps*

A single depth jump can be used as a test of an athlete's ability to use the legs to absorb shock and produce explosive power. First the athlete measures his or her best standing vertical jump. Then in the same place the athlete measures does a 16″ depth jump and measures vertical achievement. If the depth jump is the same or greater than the standing vertical jump, the athlete is in good or very good condition; if not, then the athlete is in less than good condition. Scientists suppose that in the first case, the athlete's connective tissue is strong and springy so that it can store and release some of the energy of the fall, while in the second case, the athlete's connective tissue is not so strong and the protective aspects of the nervous system inhibit the athlete from jumping high.

As a coach, I get to see the same effect of well or poorly conditioned connective tissue even in level jumps. If I ask my team to do a two-legged hop across the gym (or worse, a one-legged hop) I will see that some athletes take a terrible pounding every time they land after a hop. On the other hand some of the better athletes look like they have springs on the bottom of their feet as they hop across the floor. Springiness is an asset to athletic performance. The depth jump demands an extreme exercise of this ability.

> *When the depth jump was first used in modern strength training, experts recommended that athletes jump from high places in the neighborhood of four feet above the ground. This is emphatically no longer the case! Over the decades, the recommended height from which to execute a depth jump has descended to a range of 16 to 24 inches. This is because they have found no added benefit from the added pressure on the joints from falling so far, and certainly none that compensate for the increased risk of overuse injuries.*

In contrast to sports like basketball, where vertical leap is very useful, fencing makes little or no use of altitude. Therefore, the level jumps are the meat and potatoes of fencing plyometrics. There are many varieties of fun and challenging level jumps. Because they are vertical, the box and depth jumps are not directly applicable to fencing but they do promote an essential reactive springiness in the athlete. This springing capability comes from an improved nervous system and more powerful connective tissue. So, for body preparation for martial arts such as fencing, the box is a useful tool.

Power Clean & Dynamic Overhead Press (Clean & Jerk)

The power clean and dynamic overhead press, when combined, constitute what weightlifters call the clean and jerk—getting a heavy barbell from a position hanging at hip level to resting at shoulder level to raised above the head with elbows locked out. All this is done dynamically but safely. At first this may seem like a brutish feat ideal for "ironheads" but not fencers. But in fact, the combination of speed and stabilizing power needed to toss the weight up there and stabilize it high above the head are great stimulants for the fencer. Fencers need not strive for the massive weights of Olympic lifters, but they will achieve the speed and the stability.

In the power clean exercise the athlete pulls up on a barbell while driving upward with the legs, then, at exactly the right moment, drops under the weight and stabilizes it at shoulder level. The power clean is a wonderful body integrating exercise. When done properly, it is mentally and physically stimulating. Along with the squat, the power clean also stimulates the endocrine system, putting the body in a good chemical state for increasing in strength.

You have developed competence in the dead lift and the upright row and have learned the parts of the clean as described in Phase 1. Your posture and your abs have been prepared in Phases 1 and 2. Now that the parts of your body are ready for the stress you can begin to add weight to the clean. Now you can learn to enjoy the power clean as a wonderful expression of your strength.

Most lifters can clean more than they can press over their head. So in the sport of weightlifting the power clean is understood as a heavy weight clean that you have no intention of trying to lift over your head. (This does not mean that *you* must lift more in the clean than you can press overhead.) The power clean is a heavy lift but it is also a high skill lift. The athlete gets the heavy weight up to the shoulders with a combination of power and great technique.

> *As you progress from a lighter weight clean to a heavier weight clean have someone watch you lift to make sure your technique does not degrade under the stress of the greater weight.*

The move to the power clean is really a new learning experience as your body learns the trick of heaving up and catching the new weight.

The "jerk" or dynamic overhead press is done exactly like the overhead press described previously, except that the athlete flexes the legs and drives upward while pushing up the weight. The jump tosses the weight off the shoulders. After the legs get the weight moving, the arms push the weight all the way up. Then the lifter locks the elbows while the legs spread forward and back and grip the floor. The athlete should be in complete control of the weight when it is over the head, not trembling like someone going for a new Olympic record.

Finally you can practice the "clean and jerk" which is a clean directly followed by a dynamic overhead press. By "directly followed" I don't mean that the press must be immediate. You can pause a moment and get yourself situated for the press portion of the lift. You should treat the clean and jerk like any other lift. Do it at a weight where you can do repetitions for sets of sixty seconds *while staying in good control of the weight.* Just because Olympic lifters do single reps of huge weights doesn't mean you should try to max out on an Olympic lift.

Lift for fun, skill, and strength. In that way, you can avoid the injuries that come from an excess of pride, testosterone, or joie de vivre.

Illustrations

Section 3.1: Accelerating Leg Exercises

Lunge Jump

Scissors Lunge Jump

Step-up Jump, Straight

Squat Jump with Medicine Ball Press

Box Jump

Depth Jump

Lateral Bound with Medicine Ball to One-Leg Stand

Dot Drill

Alternating Side Hop over Cone

Power Clean

Dynamic Overhead Press

Lunge Jump

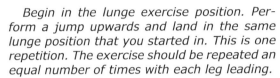

Begin in the lunge exercise position. Perform a jump upwards and land in the same lunge position that you started in. This is one repetition. The exercise should be repeated an equal number of times with each leg leading.

Keep your abs activated, a neutral spine and your front knee over the front foot. An error in knee/foot position would be to allow the knee to move forward over the toes or even further forward past the toes. Notice that the athlete in Photo 2 keeps her upper body between her feet during the leaping portion, rather than translating her body forward and over the front foot in order to get elevation. Notice also that the athlete's side to side stability is challenged on the landing (her hands instinctively came out to help balance).

This movement exercises the leading leg in the flexed knee/flexed hip position. This position works the hip extensor musculature. It also presents a challenge to balance and a challenge to pelvic and lower back stability.

This exercise is a progression of the lunge and the lunge with a twist. It adds explosiveness and the dynamic aspect of catching one's own weight when landing. As such it is a greater challenge to the connective tissue and the nervous system than the stepping versions of the movement. This exercise progresses to the scissors jump lunge.

Scissors Lunge Jump

Begin in the lunge exercise position with your right leg forward. Perform a jump into the air and land in a lunge position with legs reversed. During the jump, your legs pass by each other like scissors and you land with your left leg forward. This is one repetition.

Keep your abs activated, a neutral spine and your front knee over the front foot. Notice the athlete keeps her upper body between her feet during the leaping portion, rather than translating her body forward and over the front foot in order to get elevation. This movement exercises the leg in the flexed knee/flexed hip position. This position works the hip extensor musculature. It also presents a challenge to balance, particularly lateral stabilization. Since the rear leg is in a position to stretch the hip flexors, this motion is a challenge to pelvic and lower back stability. The negative tendency is for short stiff hip flexors to rock the pelvis forward. The athlete must fight this tendency with good abdominal tone.

This exercise is a progression of the lunge and the lunge with a twist. It adds explosiveness and the dynamic aspect of catching one's own weight when landing. As such it is a greater challenge to the connective tissue and the nervous system. This exercise can be progressed by doing the same exercise with a twist while holding a medicine ball.

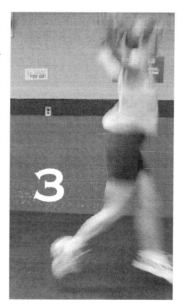

Step-Up Jump

Begin standing with your right leg on a very solid step-up platform. Push off with both legs and jump up. Land first with the right leg on the platform and then the left leg on the floor. This is one repetition. Exercise both legs.

At first, you push with both legs. Then your bottom leg leaves the floor and the leg on the step does the rest of the work. You may begin this exercise with slower speed and less than maximal jumps while you work on the proper form. Do not let the knee go in front of the foot, especially on the way up. Do not let the upper body lean forward. Stay upright.

The abdominals should be activated throughout this exercise to support the lower back on takeoff and landing.

This exercise requires strong legs and stable pelvis and low back. The athlete should have a solid background in basic and integrated strength training exercises. This exercise trains strength, speed, stability and coordination. It focuses on the hip extensors, as does the step up and over and the lunges.

This exercise is a progression of the step-up-and-over. This movement exercises the same prime mover muscles as the lunge and the jump lunge.

Squat Jump with Medicine Ball Press

N. B. This exercise should be performed with caution.

Begin standing and holding the medicine ball in front of your chin. Drop down into a squat position and immediately jump up, push the ball over head and release the ball. This is one repetition.
 Let the ball come back down and hit the ground without catching it. The ball has too much speed coming down. Trying to catch it is too dangerous. Let it drop.
 When dropping down into the squat think of a spring increasing tension as it compresses and then bouncing up. Don't stop at the bottom of the squat. The purpose of this exercise is quickness. How high the ball goes is not as important as how quickly the legs bounce out of the squat and how quickly the ball leaves the hands.
 This exercise is a progression of the overhead press. It adds explosiveness and integration and is therefore an exercise for the nervous system and the connective tissue. The nervous system learns how to summon the full explosive strength of each muscle and coordinate the firing of each muscle to produce the quick upward toss.

This exercise should be done outdoors or in a field house where there is no chance of hitting the ceiling. Also no people should be nearby so that no one gets hit by the falling ball, which can cause very serious injury. Clear the area! Pay attention!

Box Jump

Begin facing a very solid jumping plat-form with feet parallel and under the hips. Squat down and immediately spring up and forward. Land on the platform in a balanced semi-squat position, head and back upright, abdominals activated. Hop backwards and down to the floor. This is one repetition.

Throughout the whole process of explod-ing off the floor, flying through the air and landing in a semi-squat you should keep excellent upright posture. No hyperexten-sion of the low back on the takeoff. No leaning on the landing. You should land in a fighting position, head up and ready to look at an opponent.

For variety, you can begin facing away from the platform then jumping up and backwards onto the platform. The back-wards jump should at first be tried on a much shorter platform and with a spotter in case the jumper stumbles.

This motion exercises the strength, speed, and integration of the abdom-inals and legs. It also exercises a reactive springiness in the legs.

This exercise is an advanced form of the squat. The athlcte should have a solid background in basic and integrated leg and abdominal exercises. Once the athlete be-comes proficient at this jump it can be done repetitively for a certain period of time to add an endurance element to the exercise. For example, the athlete can perform as many jumps as possible in 20 seconds.

Depth Jump

Begin standing on a platform with posture at the ready, abdominals activated and head and chest upright. Hop off the platform easily. On landing act like a spring: store up all the energy of the fall and leap up as high as possible. This is one repetition.

This exercise should only be done by a well-conditioned athlete. Weaker athletes will get less vertical leap from the depth jump than from a jump directly off the floor because they are overcome by the energy of the fall. You should perfect bounding, hopping and jumping up onto a box before you try the depth jump. The ideal platform is 12-24 inches off of the ground. The ideal floor is neither rock hard nor mushy.

This exercise places demands on the midsection to stabilize the spine, on the total facilitation of muscle power for explosive drive with the legs, on connective tissue to store a high level of tension and release it for use in the vertical jump, and on integration of the upper and lower body to make a coordinated effort at maximum vertical leap. Even though fencing is not a vertical sport, the leg drive, coordination and connective tissue strength gained in this exercise will help fencers.

This exercise is a progression of squats and box jumps. It should be treated like a "heavy" exercise and given in sets with a small number of reps and with ample rest between sets.

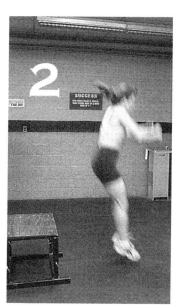

Lateral Bound with Medicine Ball to One-Leg Stand

This exercise is called a bound because the athlete uses alternating landing legs. The other sort of exercise, where the same leg is used to land after each jump, is called a hop.

Begin standing on one leg in front of a cone (Photo 1). Jump to the other cone (Photo 2) and balance for three seconds in a one leg stand (Photo 3). Jump back to the first cone and balance in the one leg stand. This is one repetition.

This motion is a dynamic stability exercise. The athlete must control moving forces to accomplish a momentary one-leg stand. In the last picture she is catching herself in the single leg stand and this time she keeps great balance and posture.

Like all jumping exercises, this movement challenges connective tissue. This exercise also has an element of explosiveness.

This exercise is a progression of basic leg exercises such as the squat. It is also a progression of the one-legged stand on a foam pad. The athlete should have a solid background in the basic and integrated exercises. This exercise can be made easier by doing it without the ball. It can be made harder by moving the ball from side to side with each bound.

The athlete can also toss the ball from the single-leg stance to a partner or coach who then tosses it back, either to the same side or the other side. In the case of a throw to the opposite side, the athlete must jump to catch it.

Dot Drill

Begin standing on one leg on one dot in a dot pattern taped on the floor. In the photos the pattern is four dots in a 36" square. Hop back from front right to back right. Then bound from back right to front left. Then hop from front left to back left. Then bound from back left to front right. This is one repetition of the pattern. You can perform almost any imaginable pattern. This is just one example.

This is a combination hopping and bounding drill. It incorporates challenging changes of direction into the motion.

This exercise promotes a reactive springiness in the legs. It stimulates the nervous system. It also challenges the connective tissue of the leg. As well it promotes integration of the abdominal musculature in that the torso must control the momentum of the upper body as it is propelled from dot to dot by the legs.

This exercise is an advanced form of accelerating exercise. It is not advanced in resistance like the depth jump. Rather, it is advanced in agility and in coordination of upper and lower body. This exercise can be progressed by performing it while holding a medicine ball. It can also be progressed by adding momentary single leg stands at regular intervals or at the command of the coach or training partner.

Alternating Side Hop over Cone

Begin standing between two small cones or markers, with knees flexed and good neutral posture. Jump to the left and land on the left leg. Hop to the center and land on two legs. Jump to the right and land on the right leg. Hop to the center and land on two legs. This is one repetition.

As you progress in skill you should try to clear the cone by as little as possible. Notice that the athlete is fully translating her body across the cone.

This combination of jumps and hops adds a side to side element to the purely front and back motion found in the squat and lunge. The sideways pushoff is very much a feature in martial arts such as fencing. It strengthens the connective tissue and promotes a reactive springiness in the legs.

This motion is an advanced leg exercise. It requires a solid background of basic and integrated exercises for both legs and abdominals. Approach it in small doses at first and test your tolerance, particularly your connective tissue strength. This exercise can be progressed by performing it while holding a medicine ball. It can also be done with a one leg stand in each of the outside positions. Finally, it can be done in combination with a toss and catch. For example, the coach stands facing the athlete and each time the athlete is on one leg, the coach tosses a medicine ball, which the athlete catches with one or both hands and returns to the coach.

Power Clean

This is an advanced exercise: the athlete should have a solid background in all basic and integrated strength training exercises. There is no way a beginner or someone just returning from a layoff should be heaving weights around like this.

Begin by standing with bar in hand, hanging somewhere around hip level, knees flexed. Do the following things fluidly in order: Dynamically straighten your legs, pull the weight up with your shoulders as though doing an upright row, push off with your toes, drop your elbows, drop your body, catch the weight at shoulder height. Return to the beginning position. This is one repetition.

It is essential that the abdominals be activated during this exercise to protect the spine. Explosive coordination is the key to this exercise.

This is a strength, speed and coordination exercise involving legs, torso and upper body.

This exercise is very stimulating. It makes the athlete feel energetic. If the advanced athlete has only a short amount of time to spend in a workout, this exercise would give much benefit.

This exercise is progressed by adding weight, reps and sets. It can also be combined with the dynamic overhead press. This combination is called the "clean and jerk" in weight lifting circles.

Dynamic Overhead Press

Begin with a barbell at the shoulders. Flex your knees. Dynamically push up with your legs to toss the weight off your shoulders. Push the weight overhead and drop your body down and move your feet to the split stance. Walk the feet in tiny steps to the square stance. Return the weight to shoulder level. This is one repetition.

This is a form of the overhead press. The added push with the legs allows the athlete to lift a heavier weight. But the athlete must not advance the weight beyond their ability to control it safely overhead.

During practice of the overhead press you must keep your transverse abdominus firm to stabilize the joints of the lower spine. Otherwise, this exercise tends to produce hyperextension of the lower spine and the resulting back problems.

This is a strengthening exercise with an essential stability and balance component. Holding the weight overhead challenges the balance and causes the body to build a very firm torso. This exercise is commonly done in combination with the power clean. The combination is known as the "clean and press" or the "clean and jerk."

This exercise is progressed by adding weight, reps and sets. The torso stability aspect of this exercise is progressed by bounding with a medicine ball.

3.2: Accelerating Arm Exercises

Medicine Ball for Arms and Torso

When you enter Phase 3, the program calls for some fairly drastic changes in how you will train your arms. The arm training in this section uses lighter weights, higher speed, higher impact, and more change of direction. The result is an accompanying need to control momentum. You should have built up your shoulders with appropriate basic weight training and stabilized them with integrated exercises such as the standing push with rubber tubing. You need good shoulders for exercises likes the Running in Pushup Bridge. These exercises are fun but they are not something to be toyed with unless you have the proper preparation. The young and the young at heart want to do these kinds of exercises because they are so active and dynamic and are tempted to skip the previous phases to get to them. But my strong advice is don't skip the previous phases.

Don't skip the previous phases just because these exercises are fun.

The exercises in this section use lighter weights, but "lighter" is a relative thing. The Running Pushup is a body weight exercise, so bigger people are doing it with more weight than small and thin people. Some who can bench press 250 pounds will be able to do a medicine ball chest pass with a really heavy ball and still get good speed. If you have only one of these monsters in a given training location it may be hard for him to find someone to toss the ball with because they can just about kill their weaker partner with the speed and weight of their throw. If you are this person you can make use of a good medicine ball rebounder, sort of a small, heavy-duty trampoline attached to a sturdy frame that you can adjust so the ball bounces back to you in the air.

For accelerated strength training exercises involving the arms, the basic tool is the medicine ball. The medicine ball is available in smaller, single-handed balls and larger two-handed balls. Size is usually associated with weight. For example, if you want a medicine ball that you can catch with one hand, the heaviest one that is generally suitable (it's softball-sized) weighs six pounds. Any heavier ball will be larger and less convenient to catch with one hand.

Medicine balls also come in bouncing and non-bouncing versions. The bouncing types are good for partner passing that involves a downward throw that bounces up to the partner. The non-bouncing balls are handy because they don't roll away when you throw the ball and your partner misses it. I tend to get the larger balls in the bouncing version and the small, one-handed balls in the non-bouncing version. The non-bouncing balls are good for single hand catching because you can squeeze them, which makes them easier to catch for people with small hands. Also, small non-bouncing medicine balls are better than dumbbells for wrist training because you can grab them and squeeze the ball with your fingers, rather than simply locking your fingers around the handle of a dumbbell.

You should recall from earlier discussions that deceleration is harder work than acceleration in the same way that lowering something is harder on the muscle than raising it. When working with smaller or younger athlete, it is common to walk the ball back to the athlete and hand it to them. This way you don't force them to endure the pounding of catching the ball as part of their first experience. First they should become familiar with handling and heaving the ball. Later, they must also learn to catch the ball, teaching their muscles to decelerate an object and deal with the impact on the arm and on the whole body.

When working with smaller or younger athletes, you can walk the ball back to them.

Illustrations

Phase 3.2: Accelerating Arm Exercises

Wrist, Neutral Position with Medicine Ball

Chest Pass with Medicine Ball

Jump Pushup onto Foam Blocks

Running in Pushup Bridge

Wrist, Neutral Position with Medicine Ball

Begin with the ball held in a neutral grip, with your fingers pointed away from your body, your elbow flexed, and your hand a little below your elbow. Quickly flex your elbow and wrist in coordination to toss the ball to about head height. As the ball descends, grab it and decelerate it, returning to the original position. This is one repetition.

The medicine ball in the picture is a brand called D-ball. It is softball-sized and somewhat soft, so the athlete can squeeze it with the fingers. Hence the motion works the wrist and the fingers as well. The ball in the photos weighs 2 pounds.

This is an accelerating exercise. The objective is to control the weight and, when throwing it, get it out of the hand as quickly as possible. This motion exercises the fingers, wrist and elbow joints in combination. It develops agility, strength and speed in the hand and wrist and toughens the connective tissue.

Progress this exercise by adding repetitions. You can increase weight, but you should not increase to a weight that slows your hand down. For variation, you can toss the ball with a supinated or pronated grip. Or you can do a wrist flex toss and catch with a partner. You can toss the ball from hand to hand. If you have access to a medicine ball rebounder, you can incorporate bounce and catch moves.

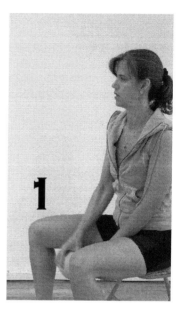

Chest Pass with Medicine Ball

The athletes begin by facing each other, one athlete holding a medicine ball at chest height, knees flexed and abdominal muscles activated. The athlete with the ball pushes the ball forward explosively and releases it. The other athlete catches the ball, absorbing its energy like a spring and immediately "bouncing" it back to their partner who repeats the spring-like catch and toss. Repetitions are counted by the number of catch/toss motions for each athlete. Each is called a touch. So, for example, the exercise might stop after each athlete gets 15 touches.

This motion exercises explosiveness in the upper body and integration with the stabilizing muscles of the torso and legs. The exercise promotes acceleration. Once the arms have absorbed the energy of the incoming ball, they get rid of the ball quickly.

This is an advanced version of the bench press and single arm cable push exercises. The athlete should have a solid background in basic and integrated exercises before attempting this exercise.

This exercise is commonly combined with twist toss to make a drill: 5 touches for each athlete in twist toss left, 5 in chest pass, 5 in twist toss right, 5 in chest pass. The bounce pass may also be included. The whole drill should last no more than a minute so that the athletes maintain top speed throughout.

Jump Pushup onto Foam Blocks

Begin in the pushup position between two foam "yoga" blocks. Partially flex the elbows and immediately push up explosively. Move both hands over the yoga blocks and land on the blocks in the pushup position. Step down one hand at a time to the starting position. This is one repetition.

This motion exercises the shoulders and arms in a ballistic fashion. The athlete should have a solid background in posture exercises, basic weightlifting and integrated abdominal exercises. This exercise is also used as a test of readiness for ballistic activities such as fencing. In this case, athletes must be able to do six good foam block pushups before they can begin fencing. This test is considered a basic proof that the connective tissue in their shoulders is ready to handle the stresses of fencing.

This exercise can be progressed by jumping onto two stacked yoga blocks. This exercise has variations, some of them very difficult. A classic variation is the clap pushup—push up off the floor, clap the hands together and land on the floor. Or you can begin with both hands on a medicine ball, hop down to the floor then pushup and land with both hands on the medicine ball. You can also jump up onto two medicine balls rather than two yoga blocks. This last variation is difficult. Be careful!

Running Pushup Bridge

Begin in the pushup position with shins on a Swiss ball, abdominals activated, spine neutral, and one hand touching one of the cones. Walk on the hands across the floor to the other cone. Touch the other cone and return. This is one repetition.

In this motion the whole shoulder is under the pressure of the body's weight. At the same time the athlete is putting this weight alternately on the left and right side of the body in order to move the hands to the left or right. As a result there is a significant twisting load that the torso must stabilize to hold the shoulder up as the hand moves. This motion integrates the shoulders and the abdominal muscles. Once the athlete feels very stable in the shoulders and spine while performing this exercise they can slowly begin to add speed.

This is an advanced arm exercise. It requires a solid background in basic posture and weightlifting exercises and integrated abdominal and arm exercises.

The difficulty of this exercise can be increased or decreased by placing the ball closer to the hips or closer to the ankles. If it is under the knees the exercise is easier. If it is under the ankles the exercise is harder. This exercise can also be progressed by adding speed but only if the athlete's joints are very secure when doing the exercise in slow form.

3.3 Accelerated Abdominal Exercises

Once you get a good look at the sections on accelerated arm and accelerated ab exercises, you will see that there is some cross over between them. Many arm exercises also use serious ab strength and many ab exercises also exercise the arms. This crossover is inevitable since the two parts have been working together since Phase 2—and even since Phase 1, since transverse abdominus activation was important to some of the basic weight lifts in Phase 1. Good questions can be raised about the placement of some of the exercises in the ab section. Shouldn't the multiplane toss be in the arm section instead of the ab section? Shouldn't the twist toss also be moved to the arm section? Sure. These exercises could easily be moved to the arm section. But the reason I kept them in the ab section was to keep a strong emphasis on abs. When all of these exercises are in one section we get a good look at the broad functional range of the abs and how they contribute to the strength of the arms. Even if your abs only move an inch, they are making a critical contribution to your sports performance.

The accelerated abdominal exercises have all the essential features of the integrated abdominal exercises with the addition of dynamic movement. Dynamic movement has increased speed and quick starts and stops. As mentioned before, doubling the speed quadruples the force. Increasing speed is like increasing weight. So begin these exercises with very light weights. Quick starts and stops put stress on the connective tissue. But this stress is a natural part of athletic endeavor. So the accelerating and decelerating parts of these exercises teach the body that it needs toughness in the connective tissue. As a result the body will grow tough. Start out with light weights and give the body a chance to grow tough tendons, ligaments and fascia before moving up to higher weights.

> *Get a doctor's permission to do accelerated abdominal exercises if you have a bad back. You don't want to shred what's left of your discs. Ask the doctor about specific exercises.*

Accelerated abdominal exercises use the medicine ball in a variety of body positions. In exercises like the sit-up toss, two athletes lie on the floor and toss and catch the medicine ball. In exercises like the Swiss ball crunch toss, one athlete lies back on a Swiss ball, tossing and catching the medicine ball with a standing partner. In exercises like the twist toss, both athletes stand and toss the ball back and forth. The purpose of all these exercises is abdominal use, so focus on the proper use of your abs to accelerate and decelerate the ball.

Illustrations

Phase 3.3: Accelerating Abdominal Exercises

Partner Sit-up Medicine Ball Toss and Catch

Swiss Ball Crunch Medicine Ball Toss, Straight or Oblique

Supine Swiss Ball Drop and Punch Up

Standing Twist Medicine Ball Toss

Standing Side Flex Medicine Ball Toss

Standing Overhead Multi-Plane Ball Toss

Medicine Ball Bounce

Partner Sit-up Medicine Ball Toss and Catch

Begin lying prone as shown in Photo 1, legs bent, feet interlocked. The athlete on the left holds the ball overhead and uses arms, shoulders and abdominals to throw the ball to her partner. The sit-up is performed at the end of the throw, following the momentum of the arms as they follow through after the release of the ball. She does the sit-up and waits for her partner to repeat the same action and toss the ball back. As the exercise progresses, the athletes do not pause while on the ground. They instead spring up immediately.

Toss the ball to your partner over his or her head, not at the head or chest. This way, your partner gets a good opportunity to use their abdominals to decelerate and reaccelerate the ball. Athletes should be fairly well matched in strength so they are at ease catching each other's throw. Don't throw so hard that it is like you are trying to kill your partner. Just get it out of your hands quickly.

This exercise integrates the arms, shoulders, abs and hip flexors in an act of whole body flexion. It also teaches a reactive springiness.

This exercise is a highly progressed abdominal exercise. The athletes should have a good background in basic and integrated abdominal exercises. They should also have a background in basic and integrated arm exercises.

Swiss Ball Crunch Medicine Ball Toss

This is a highly progressed abdominal exercise. The athlete should have a good background in basic and integrated exercises.

Begin lying with your back on Swiss ball and hands forward, ready to catch the ball. Your training partner tosses the ball. You catch the ball and sit back. Then perform the sit-up toss and throw the ball to your training partner, performing a crunch as a follow through. Use your arms, shoulders and abdominals to throw the ball to your partner. Do the sit-up at the end of the throw, following the momentum of your arms as you follow through after the release of the ball. The partner catches the ball and tosses it back again, developing a rhythm with you. Each catch, toss and crunch performed is one repetition.

It is not necessary to throw the ball hard. It is important to handle it quickly and with good coordination, and to keep the torso following through in a crunch toward the training partner. The partner should toss the ball high rather than right at the head or chest of the athlete.

This exercise integrates the shoulders and abdominals and challenges abdominal stability at the same time. It is challenging for the athlete's abdominals in that they must stabilize the body on top of the Swiss ball and catch and toss the medicine ball at the same time.

For variety, the training partner can toss the ball off to the left or right to produce a more oblique crunch toss and catch.

Supine Swiss Ball Drop and Punch Up

Begin supine with your back on the Swiss ball. Move laterally, as though doing the lateral ball roll, until the ball is beneath the shoulder blade. Start with your knees, hips, shoulders and head in the same horizontal plane. This is the true beginning point of the exercise.

Drop your outside shoulder and arm. Bring your forearm near the ground. Now raise your outside shoulder and arm and punch up. Return your forearm to near the floor. This is one repetition. The exercise should be performed an equal number of times, punching up with each arm.

This exercise works the oblique abdominals and the extensor chain in the thigh, pelvis and back. It integrates the arms with this twisting (raising your shoulder) and extending (keeping your hips level with your shoulders and knees) motion.

This exercise is a highly progressed form of the integrated abdominal exercises performed in the supine position—the lateral ball roll, the supine hip extension and the metronome roll. The athlete should have a solid background in these and the basic abdominal exercises. This exercise can be progressed by placing a small dumbbell in the hand that drops to the floor and punches up. Highly progressed athletes get to the point where they can pop up on the opposite elbow— in the case of the athlete in the photo she would have her left elbow pointing into the center of the ball and her two elbows and two shoulders in a vertical line.

144

Standing Twist Medicine Ball Toss

The partners begin standing side to side. One athlete holds the ball in front of themselves at diaphragm level. Flex the knees. Activate the abdominals. Now turn away from your partner (photo 1) then quickly turn back and toss the ball (photo 2). Your legs and torso propel the ball. The partner catches the ball (photo 3) and repeats the process by letting the momentum of the ball turn her away from her partner then quickly turns back and returns the ball. This is one repetition.

The ball should be thrown away from the partner's body so she can smoothly catch, turn away and turn back like a twisting spring. The partners should remain vertical and throw the ball with the strength of a twist, without leaning to facilitate the throw. Control all side and forward bending! If you must bend with every repetition, try a lighter ball.

The exercise works integration of upper and lower body and abdominals. It works the abdominals in that they must control the force of the ball to keep it from side flexing or bending them. At the same time the abs must be the primary propulsive force to send the ball quickly to the partner. The exercise teaches a reactive springiness.

This exercise is a highly progressed form of the twisting abdominal exercises. The athlete should have a solid background in the basic and integrated abdominal exercises.

Standing Side Flex Medicine Ball Toss

The partners stand side to side with their shoulders and hips in the same plane. The partner with the ball holds it overhead. He flexes moderately to the side away from his partner (photo 1). The shoulders and hips remain in the same plane. He quickly side-flexes toward his partner, keeping his arms straight, and tosses the ball above his partner's head (photos 2 and 3). The partner catches the ball, smoothly side-flexes away and then back, and then returns the ball. This is one repetition.

The ball is released when the hands are overhead (photo 2) and the side flex is a follow-through after the toss (photo 3).

This exercise works the oblique abdominals together on one or the other side of the body to produce side flexion. Athletes are rarely instructed to condition their bodies in this plane. The strength and control learned in this exercise is a good injury preventative.

This exercise is a highly progressed form of the side flex on the Swiss ball and the standing side flex with a rubber band. Athletes should not do the side flex toss until they are proficient in the basic and integrated side flex exercises.

Standing Overhead Multi-Plane Ball Toss

The athlete stays in one place, feet in a parallel stance, knees flexed, head up, abdominals activated. The partner walks around the athlete alternately catching the ball and tossing it back above her head. He traverses a semicircle around the athlete. It is the athlete's job to toss the ball to the partner in an overhead throw (like a soccer throw-in) by turning the hips and torso toward the partner. The feet always remain forward. Each toss and catch is one repetition.

This exercise gives the athlete exposure to changing angles. In all angles, the athlete should keep a fairly erect posture, the position of power.

In this exercise the abdominals must stabilize against the varying angles of force of the incoming and outgoing weight. The legs and abdominals provide a platform for the head, shoulders and arms to accurately follow the ball and the partner.

This exercise is a highly integrated form of abdominal exercise. It is easy to just do. But it takes a while before a sensitive athlete feels the smooth transitions of force, with the incoming and outgoing ball, that are the mark of championship quality motions. When the ball is coming in the athlete should feel the forces go all the way to the feet. When the ball is going out the athlete should feel the forces come from the feet and up into the ball. The athlete should be conscious of effectively integrating the body from feet to hands and back.

Medicine Ball Bounce

Two partners stand side to side. One athlete holds the ball head high and turns away from her partner (Photo 1). She then turns back quickly while bringing the ball down and around. She throws the ball at the ground and bounces it to her partner (Photo 2). The partner catches the ball, turns away with the momentum of the ball and raises it head high (Photo 3). He repeats the bouncing procedure and return the ball to his partner. This is one repetition.

A good directive phrase in this exercise is, "Punish the floor." Then the ball will automatically bounce up to the partner. The ball must be a tough, bouncing medicine ball.

The ball should be thrown away from the partner's body so he can smoothly catch the ball, raise it, and return it, using a springy, rhythmic motion.

This exercise integrates the upper and lower body with the abdominals. It teaches a reactive springiness. It teaches the abdominals to control posture and propel the ball all at the same time. Speed is an important part of this exercise.

The Medicine Ball Bounce is a progression of the basic and integrated abdominal exercises. The athlete should have a solid background in basic and integrated exercises. The exercise can be progressed by bouncing the ball from the twist toss position, with the athletes standing side to side.

Phase 4: Incorporate!

Making Strength Work for Sport-Specific Movements

This chapter discusses the connection between strength training, sports skill training and sports competition. Phase 4 is called *Incorporate!* because it is the link between strength training and sport-specific training. In Phase 4 you incorporate your new strength, gained from Phases 1 through 3, into your sports performance. Phase 4 is more a place in your mind than an actual collection of exercises. It's the time when you practice your sport and participate in sports competition. Here are some things to think about.

Avoid Mistakes in Creating Quality Sports Skills

1. Sloppy Practice Leads to Bad Form

When an athlete makes a particular movement, an electrical message passes through some of the myriad nerve passages in the body, firing off this and that muscle with proper coordination and force. Physical therapists use the term "motor engram" to refer to the bioelectrical trace associated with storage of a sort of memory of a movement in the nervous system.

We've already discussed how that memory is stored (p. 23), but it bears repeating. If the athlete repeats a movement, the resistance in the unique electrical pathway decreases—it gets easier for the message to pass. If the athlete tries to change a remembered movement, the brain will try to send a message down a different pathway. But the message will often slide down the old, low-resistance path and produce the old movement. The old movement will take a great effort to unlearn. That is why it is best for the athlete to learn it the right way the first time! It takes less than three hundred tries to learn it the wrong way. *But it takes three thousand tries to re-learn it!* If you hurry through the first 300 tries of a new skill and never perfect it, you will have created a good motor engram for a badly performed skill. It is now easy for you to perform the skill badly and hard for you to do it well. Athletes are always learning and learning thoroughly. If the skill isn't right it's not that you haven't learned something, it's that you have learned something, but it's a bad thing.

A quality motor engram is made by repetition that has three qualities: *accuracy, consistency, and real speed.* As stated earlier, when athletes execute repetitions of any skill, whether it be a strength training exercise or a sports skill, they should start with a movement that is accurate, repeat it consistently, and then bring it up to speed. Deviations from this formula lead to skills that are lacking in one or more of these essential qualities.

Start with an accurate motion, then bring it up to speed.

2. Excessive Resistance Leads to Slow Execution

Sports skills are speed-sensitive and therefore should not be weighted, i.e., practiced with excessive *extra* resistance, except for certain demonstration purposes. It may be helpful to weight their sports skill to show them something about a particular movement, but they should only perform it a few times to get the "feel" that you want them to get. For example, suppose I ask a fencer to lunge while simultaneously pushing a teammate with her lead arm. This adds resistance to the skill of lunging and slows it down. With hundreds of reps, this would create a slow lunging motor engram. My fencer would be able to push a large weight, but she wouldn't be able to reach the target before being parried. Nevertheless, I might ask for a few reps of this exercise. The excess resistance can be used to make the fencer feel her rear leg pushing forward. Here the weight is used to increase feedback and could be used to wake up a sleeping rear leg. So yes, I do ask my young fencers to lunge while pushing a teammate across the floor but I make sure that the number of repetitions of this "weighted" lunge is low and the number of repetitions of a regular, unweighted lunge is much higher.

Certain forms of skewed resistance may inadvertently skew an athlete away from the ideal strength balance for their sport. Imagine a boxer learning to punch by punching against the pull of a rubber band. This completely ignores the decelerating phase of the punch because the rubber band, not the athlete's neuromuscular system, decelerates the punch. The boxer has only trained half of a functional punch—the ability to throw the hand forward, but not the ability to retract it if it misses. Bench presses plus bent-over rows can strengthen the physical machinery of accelerating the hand forward and decelerating it and pulling it back. But the actual motor engram of the lightning quick out-and-in sports motion can only be trained naturally, with the actual sports implement. In boxing, that means the boxing gloves; in fencing, it's the weapon itself.

Uphill and downhill running can affect the legs in a similar way. Uphill running affects coordination by emphasizing climbing muscles and de-emphasizing braking muscles. Downhill running affects coordination by emphasizing braking muscles and de-emphasizing climbing muscles. I have never seen fencers doing footwork up or down a hill (not that a little of that would necessarily be a bad idea), but I'm including this example to show how even the simplest skills, such as running, and seemingly insignificant changes, such as the angle of the floor, have specific acceleration and deceleration components that the body learns quickly. Subtle changes in practice can lead to more—or less—accurate skills.

Studies have shown that resistance that slows the athlete's motion more than 10% changes the *dynamics* of the motion and leads athletes to change their *mechanics*. Coaches and athletes should understand that if a resisted activity, for example, footwork with a weighted vest, slows the athlete more than 10% from their unresisted speed, it has become a *strength gain* activity, not a *speed gain* activity. As we mentioned earlier, skills are composed of accuracy, consistency and speed. Taking away more than 10% of speed degrades the skill by cutting too much into the speed component of the neuromuscular memory of the move.

The training age of the athlete must also be taken into account.

> **In particular, sports movements should be unweighted for athletes new to their sport and those whose movement mechanics are still hit or miss. These athletes should develop strength with** strength training exercises **(calisthenics, dumbbells, medicine balls, etc.), not weighted fencing moves.**

3. Practicing Injured or Tired Means Practicing the Wrong Skill

Doing sports skills or strength training exercises while injured is another way to create a faulty motor engram. If you feel pain while performing a skill or an exercise, your body will work around it *even if you are not consciously aware of it.* You will inevitably adjust your form (which we assume was good before injury) to reduce the pain. The pain makes you relearn the skill. And this means *unlearning a good skill.* If you have pain, exercise with strength training exercises or sports skills that do not hurt, unless the painful exercises were specifically assigned by a physical therapist as a form of rehabilitation. Athletes should not practice sports skills while in pain unless they want to ruin those skills!

Another way to create a poor motor engram is practicing with excessive fatigue. Practicing through *some* fatigue is necessary. Athletes must learn how to keep good form and speed during fatigue. But very often, the fatigue is so great that the skill

Pain can make you unlearn and ruin a good skill.

slows down and becomes inaccurate. If this sort of practice continues for a long time, the athlete's nervous system will relearn the skill in a slow and inaccurate form. It is a misguided use of an athlete's heart to grind out hour after hour of slow form. Take rests between sets instead and make every repetition perfect. When you feel yourself getting tired, bear down and produce one more perfect repetition. If the last repetition is imperfect, stop and learn from the experience. It is best to end on a perfect repetition of a skill because the last repetition is the one the mind remembers best. End perfect, don't end exhausted.

Putting the Parts Together in a Week, a Month, a Year

Let's review the concept of progressive overload. All training, including skill training, cardiopulmonary training, and strength training, is based on the idea of progressive overload. The athlete does something a little too hard for their present condition, and over the course of time, the body adapts and becomes stronger and better. This does not mean that overloading the body by constant sheer brutality will make athletes stronger. A brutal training program will produce a sort of Darwinian survival—only a few will make it—but it is uncertain that even the survivors will be as good as they could have been with an well-planned program of progressive overload. Remember, *progressive* overload is not the same as *constant* overload.

Each phase in the program outlined in the three previous chapters delineates progressive overload. The question for the athlete and coach is threefold: how to modulate the overload during a single workout, how to modulate the overload from day to day over the course of a week to get maximum strength, and finally, how to modulate the various types of training over the course of the year.

1. Modulating the Single Workout

Over the course of a single workout, the athlete may execute anywhere from 20 – 35 sets of exercise. More than 35 sets inevitably lead to fatigue and poor performance. However, plyometric workouts, like many fencing practices, are hard to gauge in terms of sets per workout. Plyometric sets sometimes take a certain length of time, during which the athlete performs as many high speed repetitions as possible. Plyometrics is sometimes done on a single piece of equipment, such as a box, which a group of athletes use one after the other, each one going to the back of the line after they have completed one repetition. In situations like these the athlete can judge the proper size of a workout by an estimation of the number of "touches" in a workout. In this case the "touch" is the touch of feet to floor in a jump or of ball to hand in a medicine ball toss and catch. The following table gives the maximum number of touches per workout for different levels of athlete and different intensity levels.

Table 4			
Maximum number of plyometric type touches per workout for the beginner, intermediate and advanced athlete given the desired intensity of the workout. (Adapted from Jumping into Plyometrics by Dr. Donald Chu.)			
Intensity	Beginner	Intermediate	Advanced
Low	60	100	120
Medium	150	200	250
High	250	300	450

Exercise sets should be so ordered as to maximize the positive effect on the athlete and minimize the possibility of injury during training. Body parts and skills that are exercised at the beginning of the workout are fatigued at the end of the workout. If those body parts are essential for subsequent exercises, there's trouble. As we've seen, abdominal strength is essential for practically all exercises. So if your fencers do heavy ab work followed by demanding footwork, they are being asked to do the footwork with depleted abdominal strength. They will have less support for their lower back. They will risk degraded form and injury. This is incorrect ordering.

> *Abs should be exercised last so they can be fully supportive during the workout. This is a basic principle.*
>
> *Another principle of order within a workout is to put the most challenging exercises at the beginning and less challenging exercises later. Challenge comes in many forms. Exercises that present more mental challenge should precede exercises with less. Exercises in which the athlete has a narrow base of support should come before those with a wide base. Exercises that demand a high degree of skill and complexity should be done before those that demand less. Exercises that present the greatest injury danger should be done before exercises that present least injury danger. For example, you would do your squats first and your cable pulls and pushes later, because the squat is more dangerous and you want to be fresh when you execute it. You would put power cleans before wrist medicine ball exercises because the power clean is more dangerous, requires more skill, and needs a strong grip on the barbell that might be weaker if the wrist exercises came first.*

2. Modulating the Week's Workouts

Now let's consider how to order training within a week. Training guru Tudor Bompa suggests that within a 5-day week, the typical progression would be one day of 90 – 100% of maximum total training demand (the sum of physical, tactical, technical (skills), psychological and social stress), two days of training at 80-90% of maximum intensity and two days of training 50-80% of maximum intensity. These levels can be called hard, medium and easy, respectively. In terms of game intensity, we can think of these levels as follows: hard is more intense than the pace of the game, medium is the same pace as the game and easy is lower than the pace of the game. This format allows the body to recover properly, while at the same time the athlete continues to progress in skill, knowledge and strength. If athletes always worked hard, their bodies and minds would begin to break down. If they always worked easy, their progress in skill would slow and their strength would level off or decline.

Another way of designing a week that is balanced in hard, medium and easy work is to divide each source of stress into hard, medium and easy days. In this scheme, you would plan the physical, tactical and technical portions of your week separately: one hard physical day, two medium physical days and three easy physical days; one hard tactical day, two medium tactical days, and three easy tactical days; one hard technical day, two medium technical days and three easy technical days.

Then you would plan when these days would fall in the proposed six day training week. One option might be to put the hard physical, tactical and technical workouts on one day, the medium on the same days and the easy on the same days. This would make your week flow from very hard to very easy as Tudor Bompa suggests. Another option would be to distribute the hard, medium, and easy workouts so that the sum of difficulty in each day is about even. This may be better if you are teaching/learning something new and need to focus every ounce of your energy on one aspect of your game, for example your response to a certain tactical situation.

It is hard to design a day of practice so the sum of the stresses—physical, tactical, technical, psychological and social—are the desired percentage of the stresses the athlete will experience on game day. You may find it impossible to accurately fashion your practices this way. But there is a critical value to this way of thinking. It can make us ask some important questions about the flow of our practice. Are you practicing harder or easier than you should? Are you factoring in all sources of stress? Are you consistently leaving out one source of stress—for example, hardly ever practicing difficult tactical situations? Are you overemphasizing one source of stress— for example, practicing hours of footwork (a hard physical stress) three or four times a week? Are you messing up the focus of your day—for example, doing such hard physical work that you can't focus on an important tactical exercise?

The athlete can at times utilize other types of weeks. The athlete can work a heavy week, in which two or three days are hard days and the remaining days are a mix of medium and easy. These heavy weeks should be followed by a re-generation week of all medium and easy days. This combination of a heavy week followed by a regeneration week can be useful, for example, at the beginning of the season where one physically shocking week is followed by a physically slower week with more instruction and paperwork. It is also suggested for use two weeks preceding an important competition: shock, regenerate, compete.

For the two weeks before an important competition— shock, regenerate, then compete.

3. Modulating the Year's Workouts

Now let's consider how to regulate the whole year. The whole year has three parts that are related to the ancient Greek method of training/Olympics/rest. The first part is the general preparation. The second part is sport-specific preparation. This second part includes both sports training and competition and culminates in a major competition—in Table 4, it's called a "major." The third part is a time of rest and recovery from exhaustion. Table 4 is an example of a dual-cycle year of training. In this type of year you would go through the three parts twice, each time focusing on one major competition as the culmination of that part of the year. Depending on how you compete, your year can also be a mono-cycle, a tri-cycle or a quad-cycle. The main thing is to cycle through the three parts and avoid a monotonous drone of sports specific training occasionally spiced with a competition.

The competition segment of the year is more skill and mental training intensive than the general preparation. It also has physical and emotional intensity in the form of fierce competition. It may also have social intensity in that your competitive schedule makes it harder for you to properly attend to your personal relationships. The rest portion and the general preparation portion are just the opposite in that they lack competitive ferocity. They are in a sense more level, without the need for high peaks of performance. Therefore, these non-competitive times allow time for strength training and even highly repetitive sport skill training.

Some of my young athletes, however, are fencing serious competitions all year round, which means they never have an off-season in which to relax under in a routine of consistent low pressure training loads. Yes, theoretically there should be a break after the US Summer Nationals. Even if you are in the Olympics you get six weeks or so off. But for these young fencers, the problem is that the month and a half off is filled with summer camps where they do cardio and strength training and sport skill training. Then the ten and a half months of the season are a hodge-podge of training, competition and stolen moments of rest.

The US Olympic Team website has posted three articles on how to plan training over the course of the year. Two of them, one by Vern Gambetta and the other by Tudor Bompa, include warnings about the ruinous effect of yearly athletic schedules that include little rest and little time for developmental periods of training. Competitive calendars have changed since the 50's and 60's when the ideas of how to plan an athletic year were first developed. But the human body has not changed. Present-day athletes experience increased stress from more competitions and lack of time to develop the motor skills necessary for the sport and to rest. As a result, athletes are much more susceptible to overtraining and to all the physical and emotional effects it brings, not the least of which is that they begin to hate their sport.

Tudor Bompa suggests that consistent lower-level loads during the general training period lead to sufficient adaptation. With higher-level loads, the athlete's adaptation is less consistent. Sometimes the higher loads just stress the athlete out of prime physical and mental form. Hence off-season training for strength with solid low and medium-level loads gives a good base of adaptation for the high level loads of the competitive season. This suggests that athletes don't need heavy weeks during the off-season—they simply need to train consistently.

Table 5: Modulating the Year's Workout											
MONTH											
1	2	3	4	5	6	7	8	9	10	11	12
PHASE											
GENERAL PREP			SPORT-SPECIFIC PREP & COMPETITION			REST	GENERAL PREP		SPORT-SPECIFIC PREPARATION & COMPETITION		REST
FOCUS											
CARDIO	WEIGHTS	SPEED	SKILLS	REGULAR COMPETITIVE SEASON	PRE-MAJOR TAPERING	40% LOAD	CARDIO	SPEED	REGULAR COMPETITIVE SEASON	PRE-MAJOR TAPERING	VACATION

Table 4, above, mentions tapering the training schedule before the big competition that ends one part of a cycle. The idea of tapering is to remove a little fatigue so as to improve performance in the big competition. The actual performance gains seen in tests of various tapering regimens ranged from ½% to 6% improvement.

Principles of Tapering

The first principle of tapering is that the tapered schedule should be lower in volume but high in intensity. So as you taper practice before a big competition, cut out time spent practicing but keep the high speed and the highly ballistic nature of your best performance. In general a 75% reduction in training volume seemed to work the best. But some differences showed up between moderately and highly trained athletes. The highly trained athletes performed better with less reduction in volume, down to only 80%. The moderately trained athletes did better with a greater reduction in training volume before a competition, down to as little as 30-50% of their normal training.

The second principle of tapering is that tapering should be done for two weeks before the competition. But two weeks is an average number and the range of effective tapers for different sports went from 4 to 35 days. So within this range you should experiment and see where you or your athletes feel the best.

More Thoughts On Planning

Increase or decrease training volume (hours spent training) slowly. Don't leap into or out of training. Both will have negative effects physically and psychologically. Athletes who train 400 or more hours a year and then just quit often experience many forms of depression, some subtle and some strong, but all disturbing to the normal process of life. When you go into a rest period taper off your training intensity down to 40% or down to the time when you go on vacation. Don't quit "cold turkey."

Taper your training down—don't quit "cold turkey."

High levels of aerobic and anaerobic work conflict with each other chemically. Any exercise that continues uninterrupted for more than 2 minutes moves working muscles into the aerobic energy pathway and is therefore chemically aerobic. Work that uses the anaerobic energy pathways continues for less than 2 minutes and has sufficient rest between each bout of work. Short bouts of work with insufficient rest eventually add up to aerobic work. Extremes of each type of work should be done at different times of the year. So this means, for example, extensive running and weightlifting are chemically antagonistic and should be done at different times.

Most athletic endeavors require many years of training before an athlete can get to his or her highest level, and this is especially true of fencing. People with determination to overcome their weaknesses and to climb very high in their sport may train nearly year round for many years. In these cases, variety is essential for maximum psychological and physical development. Stagnation is not all mental. It is partly physical. A good athlete may have a sense of being stuck, while the coach is thinking that the athlete is not mentally tough enough to handle the work.

Coach and athlete must come together on common principles that include the right amount of variety to keep the athlete moving up. Without variety, the athlete will plateau or stagnate—get stuck in a rut. The exercises mentioned throughout this book can be combined with some novelties created by the athlete or coach. These can then be put into many possible combinations of workouts and contests. And as long as they do not break any of the rules mentioned above for long enough to ingrain bad habits in a good athlete, the variety will be helpful.

Using Strength Training during the Competitive Season

I advocate the use of some strength training work during the fencing season. There are two reasons for this. First it will add variety to the training program and therefore forestall athletic stagnation. Second, it can help the athlete to maintain explosive strength and local muscular endurance. But whether or not the athlete or coach agrees with the proposal to do weights and plyometrics during the season, they should note the similarity in form and effect of some of the traditional fencing exercise routines such as doing very dynamic footwork routines with frequent jumps, deep squats, explosive lunges and sprints. *These are like plyometric routines and will have the same effect as strength training exercises on the athlete who does them.* So the coach and athlete must know the effects of exercises that require strength and model them to produce the best effect for the given athlete at the given point in the season, regardless of whether the exercises are called strength-training exercises or fencing exercises.

Many fencing exercises are like plyometric routines. Plan them to give best results at the given point in the season.

Concentrated strength training produces a short-term decrease in speed. So if you compete during your strength-training program you should expect to be slower. After strength training is reduced during the competitive season, speed rebounds and becomes better than before strength training. For example, sprinters on a 2-month strength-training program were only 85 – 90% of their normal speed during that time. But 2 months after the training was reduced, they showed speed gains of 115% of their pre-training level. *The competitive benefits of strength training come months after it is over!*

Strength training is an ongoing process. As Tudor Bompa writes in his *Primer on Periodization*, "Continuous improvements in physical potential represent the foundation on which peak performance depends." If you wisely improve your physical potential from year to year, your potential for great sports performance will also improve. From year to year your athletic body will improve. As your body changes for the better you must, in small ways, relearn your fencing skills because you have more bodily skill to put into your fencing. Things you couldn't do you can now do. Things you could do you can now do faster. And so on.

As your body improves, you must adjust your fencing skills.

During the season, strength training still has usefulness in maintaining strength and fitness. Some evidence suggests that cardiopulmonary endurance has more staying power than local muscular strength and endurance. Therefore, it may be more essential to maintain a little strength work during the season than it is to keep up a running program for the sake of cardiopulmonary fitness. But given the added intensities of skill training and competition, strength training must be greatly decreased during the season.

The trick is to decrease time but maintain tension. This means lowering the volume but keeping the weight or speed the same. Some coaches recommend strength training 20 minutes once or twice weekly. Others suggest 2 – 4 hours per week of strength training to maintain strength during the season. But it must be remembered that many of the things that fencers commonly do during the season such as jumping exercises qualify as strength training because they are plyometric in nature. So, even the high-end suggestion of four hours of strength training is really not that revolutionary in the world of fencing. The only revolutionary thing might be for some coaches to allow their athletes to enter the weight room to do a few sets of power cleans or squats once a week during the season.

During the season, decease strength training time but maintain tension.

Now the question remains, what are the effects of these brief periods of strength training exercises? Very brief strength exercises have shown the ability to increase explosive strength immediately after a short rest period. Scientists call it post-tetanic facilitation. With strong, brief exercise, the neuromuscular apparatus is facilitated for even stronger and faster work. Dynamic work with relatively high weights and relatively few repetitions has, under experimental conditions, produced improvements in speed and strength following soon after the exercise. However, its effect on coordination and skill varied with the level of stimulation—too much stimulation caused a decrease in coordination. As a general example, one Olympic sprinter uses facilitation to enhance competitive performance by doing a 3-repetition heavy squat as a warm-up ten minutes before competition. The most important thing to note is that these very small exposures did not reduce speed.

Strong, brief exercise immediately before competition can facilitate performance.

The specific immediate effects of very brief strength training exercises fall into the following range. For moderately strong athletes a facilitation lift of 50% 1RM gave the greatest facilitation effect. For stronger athletes, larger loads up to 100% of 1RM produced a facilitation effect. After barbell squats as facilitation the highest facilitation effect occurred 3-4 minutes after effort. After depth jumps as facilitation the highest facilitation effect occurred 8-10 minutes after effort. Facilitation was also tested and shown to cause improvements in jumping, shotputting and rowing. These studies show that the stronger the facilitation stimulus (depth jumps are very strenuous due to speed and deceleration demands) the longer the rest period necessary to achieve maximum improvement in strength and speed.

These facts suggest that there is an optimal way to get ready to fence during the period 3-10 minutes before a bout. This preparation consists of two basic factors:

the strength of stimulus and the length of time before competition. The athlete needs to experiment to find their ideal method. Perhaps even jumping straight up and down repeatedly has a facilitation effect. It is not uncommon to see fencers jumping up and down at the back of the strip as their nerves kick in before a bout. But maybe it is an unconscious form of pre-bout facilitation. The problem is, if they do it right before the bout with no rest period it may have a weakening effect rather than a strengthening effect. The athlete should experiment to construct the perfect facilitating warm-up with their favorite combination of stimulating activity and recovery period.

A note of caution is in order here. Even brief heavy work, such as what might be done for ongoing conditioning during the season, also has an effect on the athlete over the next few days following the workout, although these effects have been tracked in very few studies. One study with moderate barbell exercises showed a decrease in strength and speed in the following day and a rebound after that. Another study using depth jumps (a most challenging form of plyometrics) found a decrease in strength and speed that lasted for 5 – 6 days and was then followed by a rebound. This suggests that the dynamic sort of exercises sometimes done for fencing footwork training (if they have a physiological similarity to challenging plyometrics) might be more damaging to competitive performance one or two days following a heavy workout than moderate barbell exercises. This is an area that needs close observation by athletes and coaches to model pre-competition workouts in such a way that the rebound occurs on the day or weekend of a competition.

Plyometric-type fencing footwork a day or two before competition may harm performance. Time workouts so that the rebound occurs at the competition.

Complex tactics are an added intensity factor during the season. In one case, the presentation of complex tactics into a situation raised the heart rate of participants' 20 – 30 beats per minute. In a skill training situation, when new tactics are presented, the rest periods should be lengthened because the mental pressure of the tactics will increase the physical stress on the athlete.

The fencing season has many peak demands, particularly for the high school or college athlete. This is known as an extended peaking phase. We have months on end of climbing and descending great mountains of peak performance. This is very challenging for athletes with low strength levels. Athletes should model their peaking demands based on their training age. Too many peaks too early in a career will run down an athlete's performance. The athlete must build strength before they add competitions. Also, at the high school level, many athletes compete in multiple sports, and such training could adversely affect what can be expected of them during the fencing season. As a coach, be understanding of a young athlete who is wiped out from doing too many things with too much zest for life. At the same time, be aware of his or her need for strength and allow time and opportunity to develop it. As an athlete, be aware of what you can expect of yourself and prioritize your competition schedule. Also be aware of your need for strength and take the time to develop it.

The Proper Training Attitude: Game Face and Inner Smile

For the sake of your health, you should spend a lot of your time happy! Practice smiling on the outside even if it is just a little Mona Lisa-size smile. Practice smiling on the inside also. Imagine that each of your organs and muscles are smiling. After an aggressive and demanding training session, watch something funny on TV. I have heard it told that one of the techniques the boxer Ray "Boom Boom" Mancini used to help himself balance the savage training sessions he put himself through was to watch tapes of old comedy shows such as I Love Lucy and Candid Camera between training sessions.

Work to be the best you can be and then enjoy the fruits of your labor, whatever they are. Physical training and martial arts in general is about triumphing over yourself more than it is about triumphing over an opponent. You cannot be cruel to yourself in order to speed the process of victory over your weaknesses.

For challenging workouts, get your game face on.

However, the proper level of arousal should be incorporated, even into strength training. You should get your "game face" on to do the more challenging lifts, jumps and throws. (Just remember that some people's idea of their "game face" is far too evil to be productive of either good character or great sports performance.) Use your game face to hone your approach to pain and frustration and high performance in the training room in a way that will help you deal with your struggles in real sports competition later in the year. It is also good to consider the level of arousal that precedes the maximum effort in fencing. The fencer goes from relative relaxation to explosion and back again many times in a bout. So, a set of lifts should frequently begin in a similarly calm manner rather than with something like a primal scream.

On the other hand, in a workout session things can become far too relaxed between exercise sets. In this situation, athletes are exercising with under-stimulated nervous systems and bodies that are too cool. Balance your need for relaxation and levity with the need to train your body and mind to function at a high state of preparedness. Even a relaxed training session can be done with attention to form, with mental focus, with properly warm muscles and with a properly activated nervous system. Otherwise the workout is teaching the athlete to ignore the condition of his or her body rather than to pay attention to it and always have it finely tuned before each competitive situation.

When it comes to control of the inner condition, the determined athlete should use the training session to practice mental exercises. Athletes should learn their strengths and weaknesses with regard to courage, emotion and mental function during a combat situation and over the course of a day of intermittent combat. They should learn the tools they will need to fine tune their level of determination, emotional arousal and mental function in a competitive situation. They should practice using these tools between exercise sets in a strength training session.

To maintain interest, add competitive excitement.

To keep the young, strong, aggressive people who gravitate to sports interested in a strength-training program, the coach can add some competitive excitement. The program itself doesn't allow athletes to lift with total abandon, but rather forces them to always use good form and stick to the program, even when they feel like doing 1RM's for fun rather than 20 rep sets for the sake of their development. So to add the challenge of goal orientation, the coach or team leader can set up "championship weeks." These championship weeks present individual lifting tests and recognize personal gains and overall champions in certain exercises. The coach can then design the tests to reward skills as well as maximum weight. Here are some examples of test challenges: What is the highest weight you can use and still get 20 good reps? What is the highest number of hexagon pattern jumps you can get in a given pattern in 60 seconds? What is your maximum vertical or horizontal jump? Tests can be made into pentathlons, heptathlons or decathlons and scored for an overall winner.

Conclusion

If there is one thing fencers need to learn about modern strength training for sport it is that strength training is an endeavor of skill. The athlete who strength trains is teaching his or her body to be more generally skilled. These skills carry over to sport in the form of improved performance and decreased incidence of injury. Skill is a very important part of what we mean when we say the athlete is stronger. Skill means the expression of strength in essential sports movements. Lying on a bench and pushing iron into the air is not very meaningful because it does not express itself well as strong sports skills. The one arm rubber band push is a necessary progression from the crude strength gained while lying on the bench because it is a skill similar to many sports skills. It requires a harmonious transfer of power from the floor through the legs, through the torso, through the shoulder and arm and out of the hand. In sports like fencing, the transfer of power is the same except that the power goes out of the hand and into the weapon.

The body is like an orchestra. What if the music calls for violins and the orchestra's violins are weak? If the conductor calls for the tubas to play the part instead because they are the strongest musicians in the band, the tune will come out but it will sound wrong. For the athlete, the nervous system is the conductor and the muscles are the instruments. The slightly incorrect music is analogous to substandard sports performance. And, what is worse, while bad music will not hurt the band physically (just the audience), poor bodily function will eventually cause the athlete physical pain.

The athlete and the coach must train for strength and for sport with an eye to good bodily function. When they see a weakness they can use the tools of strength training to strengthen and educate weak muscles and weak movements. Good strength training creates not just muscle but *smart muscle*. Bad strength training creates stupid muscle. Smart muscle can deal with unstable situations. Smart muscle can play its part in the most complicated movements in perfect harmony. Smart muscle knows how to act so that the joints are not damaged. Smart muscle has saved up reserves of strength needed for the athlete's particular sport. I want to fence with smart muscle.

> Strength training is an endeavor of skill.

> Good strength training produces smart muscle.

159

Appendix A: Suggestions on Equipment

The Cost of Strength Training Equipment

The prices in this section come from three web sites: www.PerformBetter.com (Perform Better), (www.spriproducts.com) (SPRI), and www.biggerfaster-stronger.com (BFS, or Bigger, Faster, Stronger). I am not specifically endorsing these sites. Rather, the sites are included here as examples of prices on appropriate products. They are good prices for good equipment. If you want to shop around for better prices, be sure that the attributes and quality of the product you choose are the same as those recommended below.

Some words about the choices made:

1. I have included a basic set of heavy equipment which includes an Olympic bar, Olympic weights, a bench and a wide-based squat rack (not those single posts that are always in danger of falling over). This will allow for the athletes to do the Olympic lifts, particularly clean and jerk, and a couple of power lifting lifts, the bench press, the deadlift and the squat. A bodybuilding gym would have a wider array of heavy stuff, but fencers don't have much use for it.

2. I illustrated some of the cable/rubberband exercises done with a cable but I've only put rubber tubes into the budget below. The cable machines are not in this budget because they are too expensive for most clubs. They are included in the pictures because many of you may have access to school weight rooms with cable lifting systems.

Light and Portable Equipment

The equipment in the "light and portable" section can be stored in cabinets or in the back of a van and taken on to the training floor only when needed. Therefore a dedicated room is not necessary for these items and they are very easy to carry around. These items can also be taken out into a field of grass on a sunny day for an outdoor conditioning session.

From SPRI:

- 5 sets of five different weights of straight rubber tubing with handles called The Original Xertube: $150 ($30 ea. set)
- 5 straps for anchoring rubber tubing exercise equipment to a closed door: $10 ($2 ea.)

From PerformBetter:

- 3 kg. "First Place" medicine ball, basketball size, very good at bouncing, very durable: $35
- 4 kg. "First Place" medicine ball, basketball size, very good at bouncing, very durable: $45
- 2 lb. "D-ball" medicine ball, softball size, soft, does not bounce: $30
- 4 lb. "D-ball" medicine ball, softball size, soft, does not bounce: $30
- (2) 24" "Stability ball plus pro" Swiss ball, burst resistant, extra heavy duty for use with weightlifting: $90 ($45 ea.)
- "Airex" foam pad: $50 (a little steeply priced but there is nothing like an Airex.)

Total for the Light Weight Section: $440.

Medium-Weight Equipment

The equipment in the medium weight section is a bit heavier than the equipment in the previous section. These things can be stored off to the side of the room.

For example the dumbbells can be stored in the dumbbell rack against a wall. They can also be stored in big walk-in closets or back rooms and brought out onto the practice floor when needed.

From PerformBetter:

- 12" Individual Economy Plyo Box: $105
- 18" Individual Economy Plyo Box: $120
- 24" Individual Economy Plyo Box: $135

From BFS:

- Dumbbell rack: $99
- Dumbbell pairs from 5 to 50 lbs. in 5 – lb. increments: $209 ($.39 / lb.)

Total for Medium-weight equipment: $668.

Heavy Stationary Equipment

The equipment in this section is heavy and requires a permanent place to sit it. From BFS:

- (2) "Super Bar- Silver Oxide" 300 pounds of Olympic weights and a 45 pound bar: $578 ($289 ea.)
- Alumalite Bar Set with 15 pound bar and large but light training weights for any situation that requires lighter weights: $189
- (2) Plate racks to store Olympic plates neatly: $98 ($ 49 ea.)
- Bench with rack solidly attached: $239
- Angled squat rack with wide base: $369
- (3) 6' x 8' area mats to protect floor under bench and squat rack and an area for standing exercises such as power clean: $375 ($125 ea.)

Total for Heavy Equipment: $1848.
Total for All Equipment: $2956.

Setting up Stations For a Strength Training Circuit

When the athletes at a club are first exposed to strength training they may need to go through three steps in their development. First, they need to learn the exercises while being closely scrutinized by someone who is experienced in doing and teaching the exercises. Second, they need to do the exercises in a group circuit training situation where one instructor supervises a group of athletes who have been instructed in the rudiments of each exercise. In the circuit training situation the instructor sets up a number of stations then divides the group of athletes into pairs. The pairs then have ten minutes to perform an exercise. This means each athlete at a given station gets 5 minutes of training and five minutes of rest during which they should be spotting their partner. Third, the athletes are experienced and mature enough to strength train with only modest supervision.

All of the equipment above would allow the club to set up the following training stations in a circuit. This circuit would accommodate 14 athletes with 2 athletes in each station and take about 90 minutes to accomplish. This circuit is just an example. Many others are possible.

1. Squat with Olympic bar and squat rack.
2. Bench press with dumbbells and bench.
3. Power Clean with Olympic bar and floor mat.
4. Supine and Prone Jackknife on Swiss ball.
5. Wood Chop with Xertube and tube door anchor.
6. Sit-up pass with large medicine ball toss and catch.
7. Standing medicine ball toss & catch on foam pad with a small medicine ball and an Airex pad.

References

These references are included to give credit where credit is due and to suggest more detailed reading and video viewing for your continuing education.

Fitness and Exercise

(1) *Fitness: The Complete Guide: The Official Course Text for International Sports Sciences Association Certification Course for Fitness Trainers*, Revised 5th Edition, ed. Frederick C. Hatfield, Ph.D., 1996.

(2) *Weight Training and Bodybuilding*, Franco Columbu, Wanderer Books, 1979.

(3) *The New Encyclopedia of Modern Bodybuilding*, Arnold Schwarzenegger, Simon and Schuster, 1999.

(4) *Precision Heart Rate Training*, Edmund R. Burke, Ph.D., Human Kinetics, 1998.

(5) *Power Training for Sport*, Tudor O. Bompa, Mosaic Press, 1993.

(6) CHEK Institute, 609 S. Vulcan Ave., Encinitas, CA 92024: the Gym Instructor Series, Scientific Core Conditioning Series, Swiss ball Conditioning Series, Program Design Series, Dynamic Medicine Ball Training Series and Scientific Back Training video series.

(7) *The Poliquin Principles*, Charles Poliquin, Dayton Writers Group, 1997.

(8) *Facilitated Stretching: PNF Stretching Made Easy*, Robert E. McAtee, Human Kinetics Publishers, 1993.

(9) *High-Powered Plyometrics*, James C. Radcliffe and Robert C. Farentinos, Human Kinetics Publishers, 1999.

(10) *Jumping into Plyometrics*, 2nd Ed. Donald A. Chu, Ph.D., Human Kinetics Publishers, 1998.

(11) *Explosive Power and Strength, Donald A. Chu, Ph.D., Human Kinetics Publishers*, 1996.

(12) *Olympic Style Weightlifting for the Beginner and Intermediate Weightlifter*, Jim Schmitz, Lionheart Publications, 1989.

Sports Science

(13) *Periodization: Theory and Methodology of Training*, 4th ed., Tudor O. Bompa, Human Kinetics, 1999.

(14) *Supertraining*, 4th ed., Mel C. Siff, Supertraining Institute, Denver USA, 2000.

(15) "Scientific Bases for Precompetition Tapering Strategies," Inigo Mujika et. al., Medicine & Science in Sports and Exercise, Vol. 35, No. 7 2003.

(16) "Primer on Periodization," Tudor Bompa, USOC Olympic Coach E-Magazine, Summer 2004, http://coaching.usolympicteam.com.

(17) "Periodization and the Systematic Sport Development Process," Vern Gambetta, USOC Olympic Coach E-Magazine, Summer 2004, http://coaching.usolympicteam.com.

Physiology

(18) *Kinesiology of the Musculoskeletal System,* Donald A. Neumann, Mosby, 2002.

(19) *Measurement of Joint Motion: A Guide to Goniometry,* 2nd Ed. C. C. Norkin, D. J. White. F. A. Davis Company, 1985.

(20) *Muscles: Testing and Function,* 3rd Ed., Florence P. Kendall. Williams and Wilkins, 1983.

(21) *Athletic Ability and the Anatomy of Motion,* 2nd ed. Rolf Wirhed. Mosby 1997.

(22) *Mechanical Low Back Pain,* James A. Porterfield, Carl DeRosa. Saunders W B Co, 1997.

(23) *Mechanical Neck Pain,* James A. Porterfield, Carl Derosa. Harcourt Brace & Company, 1995.

(24) *Diagnosis and Treatment of Movement Impairment Syndromes,* Shirley Sahrmann, Mosby-Year Book, Incorporated, 2001.

(25) *Essentials of Body Mechanics,* Joel E. Goldthwait. Lippincott, 1945.

(26) *Optimum Sports Nutrition,* Dr. Michael Colgan. Advanced Research Press, 1993.

5299953R0

Made in the USA
Lexington, KY
24 April 2010